From Timbuktu to Duck and Cover

Improbable Tales from a Career in the Foreign Service

BY

US Ambassador (Ret) Lewis Lucke

Published by Open Books

Interior design by Siva Ram Maganti

ISBN-13: 978-1948598330

Contents

Prologue

WHILE SPENDING THIRTY YEARS overseas in the US Foreign Service, and living in eleven countries and working in many more, I accumulated many stories that would never have happened "at home". These stories would leak out occasionally to my "normal" friends and family back in the US. To many, their eyes would soon glaze over and the conversation would shift to "How 'bout them Longhorns?" as they tried to change the subject. But some would actually listen, and a few of them said, "You ought to write a book." So I did, but not just to respond to those who challenged me.

My work took me to Timbuktu (twice), to places in West Africa where kids ran away in fear at their first glimpse of a person with white skin, to the scary run up to Gulf War I in North Africa, to the jungles of Bolivia and Lake Titicaca in the Andes, the fall of Communism in the old Czechoslovakia, biblical sites of Jerusalem, the passing of King Hussein in Jordan, to interaction with a few US Presidents and far too many Congress-people.

I fell smack into the aftermath of the Haiti earthquake, into the war zone of Iraq, and served as US Ambassador to the last absolute monarchy in Africa.

My take on my thirty-year career abroad? It was never boring.

Growing up, I had no vision at all of living and working overseas. I was from a mostly rural state in the South, where one's normal vision of a great life was to become a hometown lawyer, buy a condo at the beach or in the mountains and live mostly in semi-ignorant bliss about the rest of the planet.

Had I had a clue then about what else was possible, I would have actively pursued what eventually proved to be a rich and rewarding career. However, the truth was, as a kid and young man, I had no idea that such an interesting and rewarding overseas life was possible.

I didn't know because I came from a small city in a then not-so-cosmopolitan state in the South during the pre-computer, pre-Internet, pre-social media, pre-full time cable news cycle era where knowledge came from school, books and study.

Neither was I particularly connected to adult mentors or school advisors who could tap my interest and point me in the right direction. My home town, located nonetheless in a beautiful part of the world, was where textiles and hosiery were made; the culture was inwardly focused, certainly not worldly or inspirational.

My parents, both college graduates, did not inspire me to an offshore vision either. My engineer father was a former WWII pilot and had served in England, France and Belgium, but that was all I knew, and like so many war veterans, he wouldn't talk about it. My mother, who years later would fall in love with Switzerland, had never been abroad.

However improbably, I ended up in the Foreign Service, my tenure divided more or less evenly between three regions. Except for a two-year stint as a US Ambassador in Africa, the balance of my thirty-year Foreign Service career was spent with the US Agency for International Development (USAID), the agency that provides economic development and humanitarian assistance overseas in about eighty countries which works closely with the State Department.

All in all, it was a fascinating career, fulfilling and always interesting to me. Almost every day for thirty years, I looked forward to going to work. Even more improbably, I ended up at the age of fifty-two moving to Iraq in the middle of a "conflict zone" (to put it nicely), but that story comes later.

Never would I have predicted any of it.

———————

As a baby boomer growing up in the South, much of my early influence that led to an international career and a lifelong fascination with the Middle East came from attending church. As I would later tell my colleagues, I wasn't from the buckle of the Bible Belt, but it was within shouting distance. I remembered reading the HL Mencken quote that "In the South, divine inspiration is as common as hookworm." And maybe it was true.

As a child, I was intrigued by Biblical tales and by the people and places written about— Moab, Judea, Ammonites, Edom, Samaria,

Galilee, Nazareth, Jerusalem—a region that seemed on one hand so mysterious, and on the other hand an integral part of religious teaching every Sunday.

As I pondered the stories and the names of the places, I was led to ancient Egypt, Mesopotamia and the archaeology of the Middle East. By the sixth grade I could recite the dynasties of ancient Egypt and could reel off the names of scores of Egyptian pharaohs—Seti, Thutmose III, Akhenaten, Namer, Hatshepsut, Ramses II, Tutankhamun and so forth.

I guess I was a weird kid.

Though I had other interests such as playing sports, watching college basketball, playing music, Boy Scouts and a growing acknowledgement and respect—fear was more like it—of the mysterious and inscrutable opposite gender, my growing fascination with the ancient world and its partner religion(s) was probably a little strange given my surroundings. It was certainly pushing me in a different direction than my friends and peers.

When I was sixteen years old, for some reason I cannot recall or fathom, leaders of my church asked me to introduce a distinguished speaker who came for an evening event to be presented in the church's main sanctuary. Our church, a looming and simple-yet-elegant traditional place where many of the town's well educated and sort-of-well-to-do attended, had many active programs in addition to worship.

The evening's speaker, Dr. Bernard Boyd, was an archaeologist, scholar and Presbyterian minister who taught in the Religion Department at the nearby University of North Carolina-Chapel Hill, and who regularly ran archaeological digs in Israel. I was later to find out that his course on the Old Testament at UNC was one of the most sought-out and popular courses on campus.

So I introduced him as best I could and then sat down, fascinated, and listened to his presentation about his most recent archaeological excavation in Israel at a place called Tel Arad.

Afterwards, I mustered my courage and approached Dr. Boyd with several questions about the expedition. He listened and then asked me, "How do you know about this stuff? Maybe you would like to accompany me on our next dig? We normally try to take one high school student each summer in addition to the college age volunteers, so do you think you would like to go?"

To earn money for the trip, I spent months mowing grass outside a local textile mill, a job so large that when I got the whole thing mowed, it was time to start again and redo the whole affair. My parents had insisted I pay for half the cost and their friend the mill manager had offered me the job to be kind. I could at least rightfully state that I was able to pay for exactly half the entire six-week dig, while my parents picked up the rest.

We arrived at the now former Tel Aviv airport at Lod in early evening and, jet lagged and tired, stumbled through customs, with me clutching my first passport. We were then bussed to a rural area to an outdoor restaurant in a pine forest where we ate kabobs.

Earlier, during our flight, we had stopped for refueling at Shannon Airport in Ireland. The rich verdant green of Ireland stood in stark contrast to my new surroundings. We soon reboarded buses to our destination—a kibbutz called Beit Guvrin—on the Israeli side near the West Bank border where we were to be lodged in tents until the end of the dig.

Days on the dig soon settled into a routine. Up at five o'clock in the morning, grab a Middle East version of yogurt called *lebnah*, take a troop carrier to the dig site, dig, breakfast of a cucumber, a hardboiled egg and bread at about nine o'clock in the morning, dig again until early afternoon, then return to the kibbutz with our day's pottery shards. We spent each afternoon out of the blazing sun cleaning pottery as opposed to digging, as it was summer in the Middle East and the afternoons outside were too hot to get much done. The schedule made sense and we adapted.

Our dig was located at the ancient Judean site of Lachish. Partially excavated in the early 1920s and 1930s, Lachish was mentioned in the Biblical Books of Joshua, Chronicles, Kings and Jeremiah and the Israelite-era version was known as a "chariot city" of Solomon guarding the southern approach to Jerusalem.

Unfortunately for Lachish, its most historically significant events were in its destruction, first carried by the Assyrian King Sennacherib in 701 BC. Magnificent frescoes from Nineveh detailing the sacking of Lachish by Sennacherib's army are now displayed in the British Museum in London. The city was rebuilt only to be destroyed a second time, this time by the Babylonians under Nebuchadnezzar on his way to conquer Jerusalem in 587 BC. Surviving residents of Lachish were exiled to Babylon.

Years later, when I began work in Iraq, I discovered that until

1948, about a fourth the population of Baghdad was Jewish. That diaspora was composed of the descendants of the original Judean captives of the Babylonians who had chosen to remain rather than return to Judea.

Dr. Boyd was a constant force and the unquestioned leader of the US students, though the overall dig was led by the preeminent Israeli archaeologist Dr. Yohanan Aharoni. We hardly knew what to make of some of our fellow kibbutzim, but we were aware enough to realize this was a unique and perhaps life-changing opportunity.

One weekend, two fellow diggers and I decided to venture by bus from our kibbutz to Tel Aviv. Our plan was to spend the night and return the next day.

In bustling Tel Aviv we walked the wide streets, discovered falafel and *schwarma*, stuck our toes in the Mediterranean, ate ice cream from street vendors, saluted the US Embassy, slept in a youth hostel and headed for home the next day. So far so good...

We awoke from slumber in the late afternoon to be told by the bus driver that we were as near to Beit Guvrin as he was going, and that we now had to get off here and wait for another bus to take us the rest of the way. Problem was, we were in a rural area with the sun going down, no one to help, no signs, no food, no nothing. However-er, soon a file of rifle-toting Israeli soldiers walking in our direction emerged seemingly out of the oncoming dusk.

They asked us who we were and what we were doing there. At least that is what we assumed they were saying, as it was all in Hebrew. The conversation was going nowhere as all we had learned how to say in Hebrew so far was "*Shalom*" and "How are you?" Which obviously wasn't enough. "Americans," we said.

"English?" we asked.

No.

"*Francais*?" the lead soldier asked.

Ah-ha, this was better, maybe. I had just finished my fourth year of French back in high school and I thought I might be able to make this work. The soldier said—as I tried to follow and comprehend—that there is a curfew in effect. There had been terrorist activity in this zone previously and one could not be walking around after dark. Otherwise, he said, we might be shot. He pointed to his weapon. His meaning was clear.

We understood, thank God, but where should we go? And how were we to get there? Wherever 'there' was... The soldier pointed to some lights perhaps a mile away in a little valley. "Go there," he said. "Go to that *moshav*."

Good idea, we thought. No argument.

We found shelter in the local jail—the only lodging we could find—but they kindly left the cell doors unlocked and we caught a bus back to the kibbutz early the next morning.

That was the one and only night of my life spent in jail. At least so far...

A further realization: knowing a foreign language, in this case French, was valuable and may have actually helped to save our skins. My horizons were broadening.

Back at the dig, we continued to uncover broken pottery, some intact enough as to be beautiful: a bone flute one day, incense burners the next, and most importantly, the remains of an Israelite altar that matched dimensions described in the Bible, only the second such altar discovered to date. Dr. Boyd seemed satisfied, even happy. Wearing his straw pith hat against the sun, his pipe jutting out of his mouth and a dark blue neckerchief knotted around his neck, he looked like the serene and wise man that he was.

On our last Sunday, we attended an outdoor religious service presided over by Rev. Dr. Boyd in the shadow of a ruined twelfth century Crusader church. "Remember," Dr. Boyd said, "Jesus walked this land. Take advantage of your remaining time here." I took that to mean, visit the holy sites you have read and heard about.

When the dig ended after six weeks, we broke into smaller groups to see the "Holy Land", most staying in Israel proper, some venturing into occupied Sinai, others like me deciding to use Jerusalem as my center of operations.

I set out to see as much as I could in the single week remaining: the Old City, northern Israel, the Mount of Olives, Gethsemane, Nazareth, the Sea of Galilee, the Jordan River (really more a creek—it certainly was not "chilly and wide" as in the Gospel song), and the West Bank cities of Bethlehem, Ramallah and Hebron.

The Six Day War had ended the previous year and there were tensions in East Jerusalem where we found cheap lodgings, but I was fascinated by the Old City, the shops, the smells, the twisting cobbled streets, the outdoor markets and the myriad religious sites of Judaism, Islam and Christianity.

The Temple Mount or Noble Sanctuary, depending, was more than impressive and the Church of the Holy Sepulcher was overwhelming.

For the first time (there would be many more to come), I donned a kippot, laid my hands upon the Western Wall and prayed.

Since my own Christian faith had grown out of the roots of Judaism, I felt that observing this tradition was a sign of respect.

I heard one story of the Church of the Holy Sepulcher—the site of Jesus's crucifixion and burial—that would intersect with me again far in the future: since the Middle Ages, two Muslim families from East Jerusalem had been entrusted with the opening and closing of the Church each day and kept the keys to the imposing front door with them, protected at all times. A future colleague in Jordan was a member of one of those Palestinian families.

Other trips outside Jerusalem followed—Qumran, where the Dead Sea scrolls were discovered, Masada, the site of the Sermon on the Mountain, Samaria, the mouth of the Jordan River, Galilee. I also made it to the West Bank that had been part of Jordan until the year before when it, including East Jerusalem, had come under Israeli control.

Tensions were still running high among the Palestinians there, but those that I met were kind and welcoming. I enjoyed the first of ten thousand future glasses of sweet mint tea while talking happily with the locals. I had been led to believe that there was only one good side and one bad side of this so-called Arab-Israeli conflict, but I was coming to realize that it was not so simple. Not so simple at all.

I recall vividly my seventeen-year-old self thinking, "By the time I am old, I know that there will be peace between Israel and the Palestinians." Little did I know then.

Flying home soon after, our plane landed at Orly airport in Paris for refueling. Sure enough, there were real French people there speaking French, even though it didn't sound much like the French I was learning back at my Carolina high school. Again, I was impressed.

Once back home, I was a changed young man. For one thing, I had lost almost thirty pounds from the work and the conditions and almost had to be hospitalized. More importantly, I realized that though I lived in a beautiful state and town, the poles of earth did not emerge there and the planet did not rotate accordingly. The center of the universe was not where I had previously perceived it to be. My horizons had grown broader, I had new thoughts and insights about history, religion, life's purpose and my place in it. Of course I didn't have all the answers, but I was looking forward to the next chapter.

I attended university at UNC-Chapel Hill. Appropriately enough, I majored in Global Studies, continued to take French, met lots of new people and in my senior year attended the University of Lyon as part of an exchange program. To my initial horror, I discovered that my spoken French was worse than I had ever imagined, but I was speaking more or less fluently after three months of immersion.

One oddity of that year abroad was that our French counterparts went on strike for most of the year. Our UNC professor, himself French, told us, as it was not our fault, to go out and learn French on our own and to do whatever it took to learn it. "I will test you at the end of the year," he said.

So we traveled happily throughout *la belle France* with a Michelin Guide in one hand and a basket with a bottle of Beaujolais and some Camembert in the other. I remember one fine day in Provence, watching the sun slowly set over a field of lavender and suddenly understanding why Monet's paintings reflected this special kind of light.

Along with friends I even went during Christmas holidays to French-speaking Tunisia in North Africa where we visited the rural family of a Tunisian fellow student in Lyon. They dressed us in traditional garb, fed us plates of rice and lamb—I was given the sheep's eyeball to eat—and thus I had my first "third world experience."

Back in Chapel Hill at the end of the school year, though I had graduated, I decided to take one more course: Dr. Boyd's Old Testament course! It was the last he was to teach before he passed away from a heart attack at age sixty-four.

One evening while sitting on my front porch in the woods outside Chapel Hill, guitar in hand, I had a realization: Maybe it was possible to combine my new experiences and interests into a real profession—something international, using another language and interacting with another culture, doing something important that helped people, living life *significantly*.

Perhaps I would need an advanced degree to enhance my qualifications, so I enrolled in an international business graduate school in Arizona. I studied hard, passed finance and accounting, completed a final French course, started learning Arabic, and began more in-depth courses in business and the Middle East.

Most significantly, I met my future wife Joy in the cafeteria line the first day of school—she was very pretty and had a southern accent sort of like mine, and I was smitten. Also she was from Austin, Texas, a great place I had visited while in college.

Upon graduation, we married and moved to Washington, DC. I had heard about an organization called the US Agency for International Development, the US's economic development and humanitarian agency tied to the State Department that combined the attributes and functions I had defined back in Chapel Hill a couple years previously.

It took an entire year for my application to be reviewed, for me to be interviewed and then finally accepted into their Foreign Service internship program. As I waited, I took a job with USDA that dealt with USAID matters overseas so my resume was enhanced. I was the only French speaker in the outfit so even at my tender age I was able to travel abroad on official business—first to Algeria and next to Montpellier in France, where a French agricultural research institute was working with USDA and USAID on a program to assist agricultural development in the Sahel region of West Africa.

I returned from Provence to a blizzard covering Washington, DC, where cross-country skiers ruled the streets and my new wife had been forced to dig her way out of our basement apartment near Dupont Circle. She was not much interested in my latest tales of the glories of warm and sunny southern France.

But once home and opening the mail, I found I was accepted into USAID and needed to soon start my intern training program. I was sworn in and training began. I liked my new colleagues and volunteered to be posted to French-speaking Mali in West Africa.

But I first had to deal with a bureaucratic hurdle. The Latin America Bureau of USAID had decided that they wanted me. That was attractive in that it was closer to Texas and Joy already spoke passable Spanish, but I was set on Mali and insisted.

The personnel official handling my deployment let me know I was nuts to go to the end of the earth in Mali—it was difficult to recruit for Mali—when the more comfortable option of Latin American was available, but I had interviewed for the Mali job, had been accepted and in my heart really wanted to go there.

Earlier, when Joy and I were discussing assignment options and I first mentioned Mali, she responded, "Maui?" No, Mali. "Bali?" No, you wish. It's Mali. It's in the inner part of West Africa and is where Timbuktu is located. We got out the atlas and looked up Mali.

The Mali assignment was set. I needed to get a visa on our passports and knew that the Malian Embassy was just a few blocks from our DC basement apartment. I walked over ice-covered sidewalks to the Embassy with a faded Malian flag draped on the pole in front. Inside, it was freezing—there was no heat. The first Mali official I ever met, but certainly not the last, sat shivering in a heavy coat and thick wool hat. As he returned our passports with visas, he said to me a bit forlornly, "There's no money in our budget for heat. Have a nice stay in Mali."

I slid home on the frozen sidewalk, passports in hand and with a new realization: Mali must be very poor. I was soon to find out.

When I informed my new and respectable Texas father-in-law that I had joined USAID and its Foreign Service and was taking his daughter from West Austin to West Africa, he asked me a perfectly reasonable question: "Why can't you get a real job, you know, like in Houston or Dallas?"

What follows are stories from all of my Foreign Service assignments in various countries. These longer term assignments lasted from six months (thank you, Saddam) to two stints of five years each with several more of four years. Iraq and its "theatre" were sixteen months, but that was an entirely different category.

The work was important, sometimes vital, and that is the essence of what should hopefully come through in this book. I was blessed that the work was almost always interesting and my colleagues people of honesty and integrity.

My strongest intent from the start was to work hard at doing my duty in an important field that could affect real people and even make changes for the better. It was good for our country and others and if we did our jobs correctly, then maybe we could even help make the world a slightly better place.

I came to understand that this was the kind of work I'd sought. Plain vanilla living was not for me. Others who read these stories may realize that other, fascinating, important work is possible for them too. Hats off always to my hard-working and caring colleagues and especially to the international colleagues in our various countries—we called them "FSNs" for Foreign Service Nationals—who we depended on every day. They enriched our lives and enabled our professional work to have a chance at success.

These stories are from each of my overseas countries in chronological order. Everything stated is true and really happened to the extent my once sharper memory permits to now unveil. I have very occasionally altered a name or two to protect the innocent.

There are three underlying reasons for this narrative: (1) perhaps it can serve as inspiration for those young people who are interested in international economic development, diplomacy or humanitarian work as a career; (2) appeal to young people who do not want to live and work in a plain and comfortable vanilla world—other options are possible; (3) our country needs smart, multicultural and multilingual young people to work in our Foreign Service and maybe this can encourage them; and (4) I wanted to respond to all those people over the years when hearing some of my overseas yarns who kept saying to me, "You ought to write a book."

Mali

OUR SMALL SINGLE ENGINE prop plane flew low over the Niger River en route to Timbuktu, the fabled town that was a synonym for the end of the earth.

We were flying during the flood season when the Niger was swollen by rains from nearer its source in the highlands of Guinea, spilling over large areas of land that seasonally could be irrigated and used for agriculture. The mass of water we saw below created lakes and floodplains in places that had been desert and would be again once the water receded.

My companion on the trip was our USAID anthropologist, Dr. Gerry Cashion, who I met on day one in Bamako and had become my friend and counselor on all things Malian. We were designated as "design and evaluation officers", planning new economic development activities and then carrying out evaluations to determine results.

Our final destination was not Timbuktu but rather the even more distant Saharan town of Gao, former seat of the Songhai Empire near the banks of the Niger River, like the capital Bamako but some eight hundred miles further downstream from the city where we had been living for the past two years.

We had done our initial work in Gao to evaluate a rice and sorghum agriculture project, arriving once by Mali's soon to be defunct national airline, Air Mali, on their one jet airliner. We called it "Air Maybe". Landing at Gao, I noticed a beat-up fire truck racing us down the runway. One of the engines was on fire.

Gerry and I had decided after that, no matter how hard the trip was and how bad or non-existent the roads were, we would rather take our chances on driving than risk another flight on Air Mali. Our Land Cruisers were solid and our driver—the magician Songhai driver Maiga of Gao who never got lost or stuck in the sand—was skilled and reliable. However, that trip to Gao by road had turned

1

out to be a long and tough slog. We passed first through Mopti and then far-flung Bourem and Douentza. Near Bourem, we watched blue-swathed Tuaregs ride camels out of the desert toward us, and they stared at us through the slits of their indigo headwraps as we stared back at them.

Past a certain point the semi-paved and potted road ended and turned instead into washboard, and then finally into sand. For a few hours Maiga navigated by a compass on the dashboard, refusing to follow any of the many sand tracks in front of us that forked off to the left and right and led God-knew where.

But for this third trip to Gao we had an offer to fly on a private plane with a well-recommended pilot. First we would proceed to Timbuktu, spend the night while seeing what sights we could see, and then proceed to Gao the next day.

I had even tried to persuade my wife Joy to come with us, as this might well be the one and only chance she had to see the fabled Timbuktu, but she quickly refused. She told me, "If anyone asks if I ever went to Timbuktu, I'll just lie and tell them I went."

It was hard to argue with such logic. During our time in Mali, we'd had a daughter, born back home in Austin and now one year old, and she was thriving. Joy was also working with the USAID mission's management office.

When we had first arrived to start our tour in Bamako, the mission committed the supreme faux pas of not bothering to pick us up at the airport. That was certainly not a good sign, but we were too green to realize that leaving two new arrivals stranded in a new and strange third-world country airport in the dust and heat of Mali was, to say the least, tacky in the extreme. So we hitched a ride into town with a man named Gerry who as it turned out was to be my colleague, office mate and new friend. He was an anthropologist who had been in Mali for years.

Adapting to Mali and its capital Bamako had been a shock to the senses despite our preparations. The economy was in crisis, poverty was extreme and widespread, a profound drought had recently ended, disease and child mortality were high, the key agriculture sector was feeble and was dependent on uncertain rainfall and the seasonal Niger River floods.

The economy, based on agriculture, was complicated by the government's flawed policy of keeping staple grain prices artificially low to benefit city dwellers at the expense of farmers. The farmers had little incentive to sell crops to the government marketing board at deflated prices.

But Mali was colorful; it had sights and smells we had never experienced, and it was nothing like we had ever seen before. We were continually intrigued, and though we often shook our heads in wonderment at the West African drama playing out before our eyes, we liked it. We were living in a real-life *National Geographic*!

Located on both sides of the Niger River and connected by a long bridge, Bamako's downtown consisted of two broken traffic lights and two "supermarkets", neither of which had much to offer but sugar cubes, tea and canned mushrooms and jam. The real economic action was in the large and vibrant open markets where we bought meat, vegetables, and whatever else was available.

We were able to fill in the gaps with a consumable allowance from the States, if the stars aligned, if Allah willed it, and if it wasn't stolen en route in Abidjan or Lagos, and if the State Department didn't ship it to Malawi instead of Mali.

But we were doing OK. We had made friends and we entertained each other at our homes regularly. Most of us even had small pools at our residences, except in our case, as we rarely got piped-in water, we used it as an emergency water reservoir. We pumped what little city water we would occasionally receive to roof tanks for daily use, or via a garden hose to fill the washing machine. The pool was not an affectation of affluence; it enabled us to bathe, wash clothes and flush the toilets.

We had hired local help to run the household, and though we were first-tour nobodies, we could afford it in Mali. The ever cheerful Samba was our gardener who did the water pumping. Our maid, Badji, was reliable, cheerful and loyal and could do what we needed done and saved us on a regular basis. When needed, she would even tie our toddler daughter to her back in her *pagne a la Malienne* to comfort her. I caught her once preparing to clean my record albums with steel wool, and sometimes she forgot how to make apple pie even though she had been making it for years.

Badji's other odd habit was to do the housework topless. Her breasts hung like loose flaps down her torso and had long ceased to be functional anatomical parts, but such was the local custom.

I was far from home.

———————

We grew to love and admire the Malian people although our economic differences made it occasionally uncomfortable for them to socialize with westerners outside of work. Economic differences aside, we came to respect these people for their indomitable will, resilience and sense of humor.

I had traveled to most of Mali's diverse regions, from near the border with Guinea in the west almost to the border of Niger in the east. It was a diverse and beautiful place full of wonder. Desert in the north, savannah and the Niger in the middle, and a slow descent into the more vegetated south as one neared Burkina Faso or Cote d'Ivoire.

Around the Niger River town of Mopti, Bozo fishermen plied the water in their pirogues and the markets offered the daily catch of large Nile Perch, called "*Capitaine*" in French, along with many other varieties of river fish.

Our first extended field trip had been to Mali's Fifth Region and the Bandiagara escarpment where the mysterious Dogon people lived. We had arrived with the US Ambassador and USAID Director just as it began to rain—rain was always a godsend in Mali—and the locals told us that this coincidence was truly a good omen.

The amazing Dogon stilt dancers had performed for us with the unique Dogon conical huts and baobab trees providing the backdrop. The Dogon were fascinating to anthropologists due to their cultural traditions and legends, their wooden sculptures and their understanding of astronomy. The Dogon believe that their ancestors came to earth from the stars.

We had also become mindful of the real phenomenon of "WAWA" or "West Africa Wins Again".

WAWA was when your flight to Dakar flew right over the Bamako airport, while coming from Ouagadougou, but for some reason never bothered to land.

WAWA was when you had waited a year for new project vehicles to arrive, and they were finally delivered but missing the tires, the spare, the jack and the windshield wipers. And once those issues were fixed, within six months only a few of the vehicles were still functional as most had been crashed or were without the needed spare parts.

WAWA was when all your mail seemed to end up in Malawi and it took a month to get a copy of the *Herald Tribune* from Paris.

WAWA was when the city power would go off for three months and your generator had run out of diesel fuel and the office had to send a tanker truck to buy more in Ouagadougou.

WAWA was more common than other local ailments such as dysentery or amoebae, and to survive, you learned over time to relax, temper your expectations and hope for the best. Still, however tough it was in Mali, we were all in it together.

As we began our descent before landing at Timbuktu, we flew over the mud-baked town of Niafunke. I was later to find that Niafunke was the hometown of the famous Malian musician Ali Farka Toure, whose music I came to love and admire. Toure used to say, "For most, Timbuktu is considered the end of the world. For me, it is the center of the universe."

Our ace pilot buzzed the Timbuktu landing strip to assure himself that no goats or sheep were grazing on it, and then proceeded to land. I was elated to be there; I had read for years about Timbuktu as a center of learning and Islamic thought and literature, where the tombs of Sufi saints and classic mud mosque architecture defined both culture and landscape.

Gerry and I decided to settle in our hotel and then see the local sights. Though much of the past glory had clearly faded, there was still much of interest to see. We were on the edge of the Sahara and it was easy to visualize camel caravans arriving in Timbuktu bearing blocks of salt mined in Mali's far north or bearing trade goods from North Africa as in centuries past. We passed a plaque on one building stating that it had been the residence of Rene Caille, the Frenchman who was the first westerner to "discover" Timbuktu in the early nineteenth century, and who had had to disguise himself as an Arab to remain safe and alive.

Our hotel proved to be a humble place, basically a concrete and metal box set on a concrete slab at the edge of the Sahara desert. We entered and saw an empty reception desk but there was a man standing behind what looked like a bar. Hot and thirsty, we headed there first. We asked for bottled water. "Finished," was the reply. Soda? "Finished." Beer? (What we really wanted, anyway.) "Finished." "What *do* you have then?" we asked. "Nothing. All finished." The word "finished" in Bambara, the major Malian language, was *abana*. And *everything* was *abana*.

So, thinking like the westerner I was, I asked the barman, "If everything is *abana*, why are you here?" The logic escaped me.

Gerry explained again, as he had so many times in the past and would continue to do, that this hotel was run by the government, so that meant that our bartender was a government employee. He was here because it was an assigned position, and he came so that he would be paid. At least that was his hope.

Shortly thereafter, the reception gentleman appeared, so we asked if we could check in. As we dutifully filled out our registration forms, he asked us a surprising question. "Would you like a room with an air conditioner? We have only one room with AC."

Gerry and I were both hot and tired so we discussed who should get the room with the AC. Long-time Mali veteran that he was, Gerry decided without hesitation that he was perfectly content to do without AC and was happy to grant the honor to me. I gratefully accepted and we proceeded to our rooms.

I opened the door to my room and abruptly stopped at the sight of my air conditioner. It sat on the floor in several pieces and clearly had not worked for years, if ever. Besides, the windows were louvered metal and wide open to the elements. Not to mention, as we soon discovered, there was currently no power whatsoever in Timbuktu.

The Germans had donated a large generator to the city but alas the installers had failed to let the poured concrete slab on which it was placed sufficiently cure. So when the generator was first started up, it shook the slab to pieces and the generator fell over on its side, never to work again.

WAWA.

The power in Timbuktu, therefore, was also *abana*.

Gerry and I proceeded to see Timbuktu. Smaller than I thought, and most of its glories well in the rearview mirror, it was nevertheless Timbuktu, and a fascinating place. We found a place for dinner that sold roasted chicken and Schaefer beer in cans that somehow, inexplicably, had made it from New York to Timbuktu. Once we returned to the hotel and had a bucket shower, we were happy and fell asleep, ready to proceed to Gao the next day.

As we checked out early the next morning, I looked at my bill and then looked again. There was a twenty-five percent surcharge on my bill. Why? I looked closer at the bill. "*Climatiseur*" (Air conditioner) was written. I had been charged twenty-five percent extra because my room had a broken, three-piece AC on my floor in a town with no electricity! I was at first taken aback but for once decided not to say a thing. We paid, said our thanks and departed.

Maybe I was learning a valuable lesson after two plus years in Mali. To apply western expectations to situations like this made absolutely no sense and would be too stressful and likely futile to resolve according to those expectations anyway. Relax. It's Mali, and it's okay; and besides, it might make a good story someday.

———————

After two years traveling the width and breadth of Mali, mostly by Toyota Land Cruiser if we were lucky, I thought I had amassed enough experience to be useful as a Project Design and Evaluation Officer.

After a couple of close calls with Air Mali, we preferred to drive even if the roads were rutted, hard scrabble, or in rainy season underwater, than fly the mainly unfriendly skies of Air Maybe. Once we landed in the remote desert airstrip at Goundam where the passengers huddled under the wings to escape the searing sun. I had noticed that the plane's tires were completely bald and only partly inflated. When I pointed that out to the pilot he shrugged and said, "I think we can make it." That same plane crashed some months later, killing all aboard.

Practically everyone flying around the Sahel in those days had a harrowing airplane story to tell. By far my scariest moment was flying from Bamako to the far western Malian city of Kayes where we were supposed to be met by our vehicles to inspect a project or two in the region. As there was no scheduled flight of any kind, we chartered a five-seater Cherokee and took off without incident. Our pilot was a newly arrived French guy who was curiously dressed from head to toe all in black including, strangest of all, a black ascot around his neck. "Doctor Death," I muttered under my breath.

All was fine until the engine stopped running at five thousand feet. Though we were gliding along for the moment, the pilot, followed soon by the passengers, began to get very nervous. No Chuck Yeager, this flyboy.

"Where can we crash land?" he blubbered. The terrain below was hilly and rugged with no roads in sight, and certainly no air strip. My colleague, who was sitting in the co-pilot seat beside the pilot—an agriculture guy and certainly no pilot himself—held an unlit pipe in his mouth.

"Lance, what's the problem?" I asked. He turned, pipe still firmly clinched in his teeth, and said, "My friend, we are going down."

That was certainly not what I wanted to hear. I was only twenty-eight, and not quite ready to meet my maker.

With the ground approaching, Dr. Death finally fiddled with the

US Ambassador (Ret) Lewis Lucke

control panel and turned a switch, thus manually switching our fuel tanks and causing the engine to re-engage.

Up we went, finally and at the last minute. The pilot had not known that for this model of Cherokee, you had to flip the switch yourself.

This was the final evidence that in Mali, and in the rest of the Sahel, it was important to avoid small planes if at all possible.

Professionally, Gerry and I had done several extensive technical evaluations already, one detailing a wheat growing project at Dire, near Timbuktu, and another of an integrated rural development project outside Mopti. We had also evaluated a rice and sorghum project outside of Gao, east of Timbuktu. Among our many findings was that the project, however well intentioned, had failed to meet its production goals as a water-controlling dike, and that polders were not well maintained and uneven leveling of the fields made for poor water distribution that often drowned early stage rice seedlings. This was one example of a project with disappointing results, but there were an equal number of successes too.

Outside Gao, in a small village, we met a Malian old man who told us he had served in the French Colonial Army during World War I and had fought at the battle of the Somme.

Gao, like Timbuktu and the entire northern region of Mali, was much later overrun by Al-Qaeda and various other rebel factions, disrupting the tranquility that had once pervaded this hot, slow-moving region of Mali.

During our years in Mali, I was able to travel to Mali's Fifth Region many times for work. Mopti was the big town on the Niger River with its distinctive mud mosques. The smell of recently caught and drying river fish filled the air with pungent smells. The town of Sevare was several miles from Mopti and near a huge and empty airfield that had been built by the Soviet Union, we were told, to be used to ferry Soviet military forces further south in the case of a future East-West conflict.

Our first trip to the Fifth Region was with the American Ambassador and her escorts and vehicles as well as my USAID boss. We had several new and ongoing projects in the zone—the largest a "integrated rural development" one where we had just received delivery of brand new project trucks and other vehicles. Knowing about WAWA, I wondered how well these vehicles would be maintained and how long they would last.

Traveling with our distinguished female Ambassador was a great experience. She went everywhere, ate what was offered to us in the villages and had an indomitable positive spirit. It was always quite a show when our convoy pulled into a new village—dancers went into action, village elders crowded around to greet us (gifts were provided, usually tied-up clucking chickens and once a sheep that we placed in the rear of our Landcruiser before proceeding down the vehicle tracks of the Fifth Region to the next village).

One village took the celebration a bit too far—at least we thought so at the time. Village men were aiming old rifles to the sky and firing them with great gusto amid the dancing women and little kids racing after us. Was it my imagination or were the shooters sometimes pointing their rifles at us while being careful to shoot them finally into the air? Gun safety classes might have been appropriate.

Entering one larger town, as we pressed on into Dogon country, it began to rain hard. The crowd on both sides of our vehicles burst into leaps and dances and basically seemed to go nuts. That was a propitious and most positive omen, to be seen as help in bringing the rain to these dusty villages which were totally dependent on rainfall for life-preserving agriculture. Of course we had nothing to do with it raining, but we were happy to take some of the credit. Timing was everything.

The town of Bandiagara was a center of Dogon activity and culture. Distinctive conical Dogon huts dotted the landscape, and it was clear we were in a special and unique place. *National Geographic* come to life right in front of us.

The Dogon had long fascinated anthropologists with their unique cultural practices and beliefs. Dogon elders would tell you with no hesitation that their ancestors had come to the Fifth Region from the stars, and they even told us which star—Sirius B—which is invisible to the human eye.

To complete the welcome, Dogon dancers dressed in red costumes and wearing distinctive black Dogon masks danced high upon stilts. They made quite an impression on our little group of wide-eyed foreigners.

"Best show in Africa," said my boss. He was probably correct.

9

Subsequent trips to the Fifth Region were more down in the trenches than traveling with the Ambassador. We would bring almost all our provisions and camp out at night, and then bounce down the rough tracks of Dogon country in my colleague's yellow Toyota pickup truck.

My colleague, Phil, worked for ICRISAT—an agriculture research institute for the semi-arid tropics—and his project aimed to develop, test and disseminate more drought resistant strains of sorghum and millet, the main food staple for many Malians.

If this project succeeded lives would be saved by freeing many poor Malians from the cycle of drought, hunger and even starvation that often plagued this part of the Sahel.

This was important work, and Phil and his co-workers were diligent in their field trials. Though the rewards came through slow and detailed work in the lab as well as in the field, it was exciting to know that success could be seen in greater food production and security, as well as improving the lives of some of Mali's most vulnerable.

We worked hard. It was hot, the people were poor, and the work was challenging. Back in Bamako, we would get excited if the ice plant worked and we could buy ice, or if we could score peanut butter from a colleague with a supply. Given the challenges of daily life, even for expatriates, I was soon to conclude that this type of work was more appropriate for those of us in our twenties or thirties rather than older workers. Yet, plenty of our colleagues were in fact older, and good health could more or less be maintained by following a few essential practices: drink only boiled or filtered water; soak vegetables in water containing a little bleach to kill parasites; take your malaria medicine regularly; get all your shots, and be careful of what you ate.

One needed to follow this regimen and stay out of hospitals—they were a place to die, not to be healed. For that reason, all expectant expatriate women—and we had more than a few then—went home to the US to give birth. Thus, our first daughter was born in Austin and she and Joy stayed there for several months before making the trip back to West Africa.

We did have non-work diversions: our Mali team actually won the annual WAIST (West Africa International Softball Tournament) held back in Dakar. Our team was named the "So-So Mali Beaux". "Somal-ibo" was the name of the local beer that only came in one liter bottles. "Mali" was where we lived and "*Beaux*" meant in essence, "Good Looking Guys" in French that we added for fun. "So-So" was how we rated our softball prowess, at least until we won the tournament.

Back in Dakar after a few years in Mali, it was laughable that we had once considered Dakar to be "so African". With its beaches, seafood, constant electricity and bounty of France in the supermarkets, we shook our heads in wonderment, and filled our coolers with frozen shrimp to haul back to Bamako.

After three plus years of work in Mali, Gerry and I had one major task and adventure left to us. Our Washington, DC-based boss had pledged that USAID would design and implement a resettlement project for 12,000 rural Malinke villagers in far western Mali to escape the impoundment area of a new dam to be constructed on the Bafing River.

The new dam at the village of Manantali would be the upriver dam that would permit controlled year-round irrigation water and also a source of power production as part of a larger economic development scheme being led by a multi-state organization (Mali, Senegal, Mauritania) called the OMVS, the Senegal River Development Organization. There would be a second anti-intrusion dam nearer to the mouth of the Senegal River that would prevent salt-water flow up river in the dry season, thus permitting year-round agricultural cultivation and increasing farm income. At least that was the plan.

We viewed this commitment with much trepidation. A review of the literature on forced resettlement in Africa showed that none of these efforts had been successful, and in some countries had proven to be downright disastrous.

To do this right, we needed to study past efforts elsewhere, compile a thorough "lessons learned" list, plan in a detailed way accordingly, and get all of our many bosses, other donors and most importantly in this case the Government of Mali to approve. This was not going to be easy and the project was rife with potential pitfalls.

What if the Government didn't provide enough help and approval; what if we planned it wrong; what if we didn't have sufficient funds; what if the affected local population rebelled? What if we didn't finish in time and the people had not moved before the dam was finished and the waters rose in front of their eyes, destroying villages, livestock, agriculture, and livelihoods?

We could be treading close to *60 Minutes* territory. I could almost hear Steve Kroft saying, "Now tell us, how could you possibly let this disaster happen? How could you have failed so badly in planning and implementation? How is it you left these people to tread water?"

So, this project was likely not "career enhancing" but to Gerry and to me fell the initial design responsibility.

Among the many "lessons learned" we studied, one was to plan with sufficient time in advance. There was a lesson from Mali's Selingue dam resettlement program that planning and execution had been compressed into far too short a time period and that insufficient rebuilding materials had been available to rebuild new dwellings.

Also, the villagers themselves had to be involved and consulted every step of the way, for example in choosing where they wanted to resettle and not leave it up to outsiders. As part of that, we needed to understand more about each of the forty-five villages and hamlets affected. Questions of kinship, livelihood, religious beliefs, women's issues, the need to firmly reestablish livelihoods before getting too innovative and knowledge of alternate sites were key factors.

Another was that the Malian government had to be a full participant and co-leader—it was their country, after all—and at least devote personnel to the project from the start. We soon identified our first key Malian counterpart, a young hydrological engineer named Robert Dembele. We liked him from the start.

So began a year-long design effort that involved sojourns to Mali's First Region and the Manantali zone. We drove our two Land Cruisers the long distance near the railroad tracks past Bafoulabe and head south on rough dirt tracks to Manantali and then to our preferred campsite at the small village of Keniekenieko on the banks of the Bafing, a tributary of the Senegal.

By our second trip to Keniekenieko, we had built a tent camp complete with an outdoor sun-shower with straw walls, bringing a camp cook and soon developing a habit of hunting our own dinners with our shotguns in the form of pheasant and guinea fowl. We really wanted to jump into the Bafing but the fear of schistosomiasis and hippos kept us dependent on the sun-shower.

We had hauled our gasoline on roof racks that Gerry had designed and installed on the vehicles and tried to preserve baguettes from Bamako in large plastic bags. We even found an American missionary who offered to put beers in his kerosene refrigerator. That part was likely not in his "Missionary Handbook" so we doubly appreciated the gesture.

The camp was comfortable enough but we were still in the middle of nowhere in one of Mali's most isolated zones. We even had village children run away in abject fear at first sight of us: they had never seen white people and apparently thought we were ghosts. As the children fled, their parents broke into gales of laughter. Once again, we were reminded how remote this little corner of the world really was.

We were also unable to communicate with the mission in Bamako or the outside world as the long-range radios on the Land Cruisers refused to work. As we were some twenty years away from reliable cellular, sat phones and cell towers, we had to be careful to avoid hurting ourselves or getting sick.

Our field research continued as we bounced from remote village to remote village. Hotshot Bambara-speaking Gerry did most of the talking with the village councils as I took notes, and I would chime in when we found a good French speaker.

We discovered that some villagers had been told about the coming dam and had already discussed where they wanted to resettle. In one village meeting, as we sat around in a group in old wicker chairs and on fallen tree trunks, the elder told us, "Yes, we heard about the dam a few years ago, but we have one problem: we don't know what a dam is."

To myself I thought, "This might be hard."

Gerry, however, was nonplussed. He pointed high up on a nearby cottonwood tree—a bit dramatically I thought—and said in Bambara, "A dam is a wall that will block the river and make a lake as deep as the top of this tree."

That was clear enough and the folks got the message.

After months of this kind of survey work, we had made much progress, figured out the who's who of the zone, spread the definitive word of the coming dam, better understood which village wanted to move where and in the case of the need of village amalgamation for purposes of economy, who would be willing to move in with whom.

As we gathered this info about villagers' views of other villages with whom they would be willing to settle in new sites, there was one village that nobody wanted to integrate with. Nobody!

"What's the problem with that place?" we asked. "They are sorcerers," was the answer. "Okay," we responded, "we'll amalgamate the other villages and leave that one alone."

This was all valuable preliminary work but we realized that to do this right a new and more detailed follow-on survey, this time with

13

government representatives, was needed. We were determined with the means at our disposal to do this one forced resettlement right, or at least as right as one such project—almost by definition with a negative prognosis—could possibly be done.

I went to Washington to present the preliminary plan to the home office, and it was approved.

One DC wag asked, "Wouldn't it be better to just give them bus tickets to Dakar?" Since there were no buses and no roads, I finally got that this was a joke but I was minimally content that we were starting to know what we were doing, at least far better than when we began.

Gerry and I continued to work on the Manantali resettlement design back in Bamako while other donors began to work on other portions of the project—clearing the dam site of vegetation, building a workers' camp, and even constructing a real road from the railhead down to Manantali village and beyond.

I actually flew alone back to Manantali on a Malian troop plane—nervously glancing at my watch every thirty seconds to calculate how much time the plane needed to go to our destination without falling out of the sky—to attend the project inauguration ceremony headed by the Presidents of Mali, Senegal and Mauritania, the members of the OMVS.

Abdou Diouf, the President of Senegal, and about six feet, seven inches tall, was dressed in a dark business suit (a la Nixon), while Moussa Traore of Mali and his Mauritanian counterpart came dressed in traditional garb. A banner read "Fifty-seven villages and hamlets will sacrifice their land for the good of the project and country."

True enough, but I doubted this would have been their first choice.

What really struck me most, however, was the brand new Manantali road. It was wide, level and with shoulders, and though still dirt, built to European standards by Germans.

Where once we had bounced for hours and hours on horrible and almost impassable tracks, we could now zoom down the road at high speed and arrive at our destination within minutes instead of hours. There were even German-style road signs marking village turn-offs, just like the Autobahn but right in the middle of one of Mali's most isolated regions.

"*Mein Gott!*" I thought to myself, shaking my head.

I had almost reached four years—two tours—in Mali. In my trips to Dakar to confer with the OMVS office of USAID there, we had become acquainted and mutually appreciative of the help we could provide each other. At the end of my last trip there, the USAID office chief asked me about my future plans and whether I would like to be considered for a position in the Dakar office.

Dakar was the ultimate good post for us isolated Sahel hounds working in places like Bamako, Niamey, Nouakchott or Ouagadougou. In fact, it was the African version—as far as I knew at the time—of Paris.

The State Department folks had Paris, London, Bern, Copenhagen and so forth as prime posts. The USAID folks (and we preferred it this way because this was our chosen field) could hope for Dakar with its beaches, sea breezes, interesting culture and history, French comforts, and its own development challenges. So, after discussions with my spouse, boss of USAID/Mali and the official approval of everyone necessary, I was assigned to Dakar.

My wife and daughter made plans to move from Bamako to Dakar via Air Afrique. I, however, had chosen a different route. We wanted to keep our relatively new Peugeot, so I decided to sit in my car on a flatbed railcar for the entire distance from Bamako to the first city in Senegal, Tambacounda, where the paved road to Dakar started and where I could leave the train.

It would be a long and hot trip, but yet another adventure. I could theoretically make it to Tambacounda in about eighteen hours, if the train didn't break down, and my car not diverted to a siding rail, if I was not robbed, if God willed it, and if major WAWA did not happen.

I packed my shotgun under the seat just in case, along with as much water and other drinks, including one-liter bottles of beer, of course, and some snacks. To my relief, when I went to the station to survey the car arrangement, I was relieved to see that the car was pointing forward, however fitting it may have been to back into Senegal. I found there was even another vehicle strapped to my flat bed, and soon two rather grizzled older French guys emerged from the station and boarded the train as well. I would have company.

Goodbyes were hard, and after almost four years we had new friends for life, an abundance of professional experience I could never have previously imagined, good memories from all parts of Mali, a new perspective on life and development, and a newfound satisfaction with my chosen career.

15

Joy and I were particularly worried about a young Iranian couple with a toddler daughter whom we had befriended. This was soon after the Iranian Revolution, the hostage situation and Ayatollah Khomeini, and our friends found themselves to be people without a country. They could not get a visa for the States, where they had lived and been schooled, and they dared not go back to Iran. They were stuck in Mali, and this worried us—and them! Saying goodbye to them was particularly poignant.

As I began to look at Mali in my rearview mirror, I realized that I now knew much better professionally what I was doing than when I'd started. True, we had experienced some bad moments, but also much good in Mali, and I knew for the first time that I was on the right career track.

Another aspect of this job: it was fun.

So, with me sitting inside my Peugeot, and the train pulling out of the station, we passed some of my old haunts, like the tennis courts where I had actually made it to number two player in the country, past a new neighborhood where friends lived, past a new restaurant complex on the west side of town, and then past traditional thatched roof round houses, transitioning gradually into an increasingly rural Mali of baobab trees, rust-colored laterite roads and fewer and fewer people in sight.

The sun set, the heat was not unbearable as long as we kept moving, the train hadn't broken down, and it was now out of my hands anyway. I opened a bottle of beer, surveyed the countryside and relaxed. Eventually, I lowered the Peugeot front seat as much as possible and tried to sleep.

It was not a fitful sleep, but I awoke early the next morning to see that we had stopped in the town of Kayes, the capital of Mali's western-most First Region and, as I had been told, Planet Earth's hottest continually inhabited city.

I was afraid of leaving the car to seek shelter out of the heat so I remained where I was, windows down, of course, but sweating in the blistering heat. Little boys stared at me from the tracks and asked if they could get me anything. Ice, I said, which was soon delivered in clear plastic bags, and I held it to my brow and then placed the bag in my cooler. When I asked the railroad employees who walked by when we would be departing, the answer was always the same, *"Toute de suite, toute de suite!"*

After hours of *"toute de suite"* we finally pulled out of Kayes with a lurch, and at least I could finally get a breeze. I was drained by the heat of Kayes and prayed we had no more delays. By the time the afternoon was waning and dusk approached, we were behind schedule.

We had stopped again, and there was some commotion at the head of the train. Was this the border with Senegal? I could see that our train was now on a side rail and no longer on the main track.

Soon, a Malian official arrived and asked to inspect our papers. The two French guys went first and apparently had everything in order as he soon proceeded to me. I provided my passport and all the documents that the office back in Bamako had given me. After some minutes of inspecting my small pile of documentation, the Malian asked me where my other customs document was. My heart sank as I had given him all the documents I had. Our management office had made the arrangements and I had assumed that all was in order.

I told the truth to the official—though he was dressed in a traditional Malian shirt open on the sides and not a uniform: "This is all I have."

To my horror, he told me I could not pass the border without the required form, and to accentuate that fact he proceeded to unhook our flatbed car from the rest of the train. My two French cohorts in the next car, listening to the conversation, were apoplectic. They had no interest in being in this situation. Their paperwork was in order. I was the bad guy here, but what to do?

I couldn't communicate with my Bamako office to get the right document—that would require me to return there and that was impossible. My family was arriving in Dakar soon and I had to meet them. I had no way to communicate with anyone on the outside.

I had heard horror stories of cars being unhooked from the Senegal train. They could sit on the side rail for days and weeks. It was too hot, the water was about gone. This situation had to be resolved here and now.

The official did not sound sympathetic. After all, it was my side that had been unprepared. He further terrified me by saying that the rest of our train would be underway as soon as the freight train going in the opposite direction passed. Ironically, he said it was a train filled with equipment and material for the Manantali dam, which had been my focus for the past year.

Soon I heard the sound of an approaching train—the Manantali one! Panicking, I said, "Look, we can't be left here. I fully admit it is my fault not having all the right paperwork, but maybe we can work this out. I will give you 20,000 CFA now, and you can work out the paperwork here at the border. If that's not possible, you keep the money and I'll get the paperwork done and sent to you once I am in Dakar."

I was in part offering him a "commission" that would not automatically be seen as a bribe and would let him save face, if in fact he was worried about that. I had never offered a bribe before and never would again, but I was close to desperation.

To make matters worse, the Manantali train was thundering by on the other track. I was almost out of time and our flat car was still unhooked from the rest of the train. The Malian looked at me and said, "No, *monsieur*, I do not want your money."

My God, what a time to run into a totally honest man! The Manantali train was almost past. It was now or never.

Looking at me intently, the honest Malian went to the front of a railcar and re-hooked us to the train. Three seconds later, there was a lurch and we moved forward.

As we slowly advanced past the last Malian official, I stood by my car with the door open staring back in profound gratitude at the honest Malian as he stared intently back at me.

Mali was behind me. Senegal lay ahead.

———

Note: On Manantali resettlement, the detailed design was eventually soon completed and actual implementation began two years after, albeit in stages. Contracts were signed, advisors were assigned, and the Mali government set up and staffed a Manantali Implementation Unit. The dam was completed five years after our initial design work and soon villagers began moving to their new sites.

There were inevitable issues and delays like the clearing of new agricultural fields, provision of sufficient building materials and proper distribution of farm land, but two years after the dam was finished, 100% of the villagers had been relocated to their new sites and reestablishment of livelihoods and means of production slowly but surely came to pass.

With the completion of the dam and its accompanying new roads, the former isolation of the Manantali zone was finished and a vibrant new market at Manantali was established. Cash available from dam construction further transformed the economy and abundant rains in the immediate years after resettlement further eased the transition.

Forced resettlement is a complex and controversial undertaking but the project was duly completed with twelve thousand Malinke villagers resettled in their new sites.

One US anthropologist wrote nine years after actual resettlement began, "It is possible to make the argument that the Manantali resettlement project was the most successful, large-scale involuntary resettlement project ever completed in a developing country. I attribute this to a very sound design that sought to apply many of the lessons that had been learned during less successful re-settlements, and to the extraordinary hard work and commitment to making the project successful by people in the Manantali Resettlement Project Unit like Djibril Diallo, Mamadou Sidibe, Yacouba Coulibaly, Robert Dembele and many others."

Senegal

WHEN JOY AND I had first arrived in West Africa en route to Bamako almost four years previously, we had stopped and spent the night en route in Dakar, planning to take Air Afrique on to Bamako the next day.

The Dakar hotel recommended by a friend was a nightmare—Joy refused to take off her clothes—but the daytime scene was fascinating. "It's so African" we said to each other.

The women were tall and many dressed in elegant boubous. The outdoor markets were bursting with activity. Since we were on a peninsula jutting west, the sea was right there. We noted we could still find the fineries of France—croissants in the shops, wine and French cheese, seafood for sale on ice in the markets. A further cornucopia of West Africa-appropriate staples and wares was available in the open outdoor markets.

We were wide-eyed at the newness of it all—until we arrived in Bamako. Then we understood what a more original, unaffected and more basic Africa looked like.

When we returned to Dakar from Bamako for the annual West Africa International Softball Tournament ("WAIST") a year into the Bamako assignment, we had to laugh at our prior naiveté. Compared to Bamako, Dakar was Paris.

My new USAID/Dakar assignment was in the River Basin Development Office mostly devoted to Senegal and Mauritania-based OMVS projects that of which Manantali Resettlement was part. I was the only USAID person to work on something else, OMVG, the Gambia River Basin Development project. The OMVG organization, based in Dakar, included eastern Senegal, the Gambia, upper Guinea and Guinea-Bissau.

My job was "project officer" in charge of managing the people and contracts within the project, solving problems, assuring progress according to plans and benchmarks, supporting our contractors ("implementing partners" was the PC term and actually a better description) as they went about the business of implementation.

OMVG was very much in a design phase though the overall plan was ambitious. As with OMVS, the eventual plan was to develop vast agricultural schemes in the region through improved water management. In plain talk, that meant the construction of two dams was envisioned, one a salt intrusion dam near the mouth of the Gambia River and a second downriver impoundment dam to form a lake for both irrigation water control and power production. This was similar to the OMVS scheme and highly dependent on two things: positive feasibility studies and the availability of hundreds of millions of dollars from the World Bank, and likely Middle East donors as well.

USAID had pledged to undertake the socioeconomic and environmental feasibility studies—aquatic ecology, terrestrial ecology, water associated issues including disease, and rural development needed as basic information. The reports were designed to cover the entire zone and help OMVG develop as an institution. Most importantly they would prove or disprove the feasibility of the initial dam scheme, evaluate negatives and positives, form the basis for more detailed planning and decision making, and see what needed to be adjusted or mitigated in the process. We also planned to undertake detailed aerial photography of the zone to produce topographical maps that could also be used for planning purposes, particularly for agricultural development schemes. Our main implementing partner was the University of Michigan's Great Lakes Research Laboratory.

Most USAID projects worldwide had project vehicles. We had more than a few of these too but we were the only project I know of then or later that had an actual project ship. The UM folks had sailed an eighty foot research vessel, the *Laurentian*, from Lake Michigan across the Atlantic to the Gambia River to use as a research lab. Ha, we had a project ship!

The UM team was based in the Gambian capital of Banjul in the center of the OMVG states and nearby to the Gambia River. Gambia was and is the smallest country on the African continent and, as we used to joke, more or less a tow-path on either side of the Gambia River and another monument to the long past colonial struggle for footholds in West Africa between the French and British. France had Senegal and the Sahel except for Gambia plus Cote d'Ivoire; the British had Gambia and a string of states further south like Sierra

Leone, Ghana, Nigeria and so forth, though since the early sixties these were now all independent countries.

For me this meant a constant drive from Dakar south to the Gambia River and then a ferry ride across the wide river mouth and then the rest of the way into Banjul. The state of the ferry was always an adventure. Sometimes we waited for it forever, sometimes it broke down, and sometimes it just didn't appear. WAWA!

The Banjul suburb of Fajara became my second home and the UM team soon plunged headlong into the research and field work. The beaches of Fajara and Serrekunda were not bad either.

For me, the work situation was perfect. Since it was my job to support, understand and facilitate the team's work, I got to work closely with the UM team—excellent professionals and nice folks—and travel almost the length and breadth of the basin with them, seeing and experiencing everything from the far end of Gambia, overland through the Futa Jallon mountains to Labbe in Guinea, to Conakry, and down far-off tributaries of the Gambia in Senegal and Guinea, and much more.

On the drive to Labbe, the mountainous roads were so rough to non-existent that I went almost a whole day without shifting out of four-wheel low. Passing one isolated village, the entire population seemed to run out to see me crawl by. When I stopped to speak to them, one man told me that I was the first vehicle in six years to pass them on this road.

This was in an era when the quality and durability of American cars were suspect, and I was in a 4-wheel drive Blazer. Given my isolation, I prayed that if there were saints in charge of automotive issues, that they smile in my direction and keep my worrisome carburetor clean enough to keep going.

Except for my constant worries about breaking down, it was an almost serene setting—green hills and low mountains that looked to me a lot like eastern Tennessee or western North Carolina, except my homeland lacked the Fulani villages with conical huts that I kept passing, not to mention monkeys in the trees.

Guinea was a more mysterious and inscrutable country to me than Senegal—off the beaten track, politically more isolated and still run as a one-party government headed by the old anti-colonial despot, Sekou Toure. Toure was an aging West African strong-man who was well known for his anti-West, pro-socialist politics though he was now an old man and apparently mellowing a bit in his dotage, thus

Guinea's membership in the OMVG and some additional openings to the outside world.

After independence from France—a process that was ill-willed and rancorous—Toure cozied up initially to the Soviet Union. The story went that among the Soviets' early foreign aid shipments was a product that Guineans would likely rarely ever need—snow plows.

I had been twice down to the dilapidated and hang-dog capital city of Conakry to meet with Guinean officials about the OMVG and our project. We also realized we needed to set up a regional office in the northern region of Guinea in Labbe to coordinate our field work and act as a temporary project hub.

Conakry was even more underdeveloped than Bamako but set in an otherwise semi-attractive setting by the sea. I had a USAID friend who was posted there and Bobby took me under his wing and showed me the ropes.

Foreign visitors to Guinea were not supposed to change money at the unofficial rate but not to do so would have made even rudimentary vegetable shopping beyond any expat's financial reach. On the other hand, exchanging at the non-official street rate made everything more or less affordable, though the offerings of the local market were often pretty basic indeed.

With Bobby and his wife Ada, we went out to dinner in a local restaurant one night which necessitated hauling a large paper bag full of local currency to pay the bill. The currency was called the Syli which we quickly decided was better named the "Silly" given its worthlessness.

Bobby told me that one of the Conakry neighbors was the former Black Panther Stokely Carmichael who had taken up refuge in Guinea, changed his name to Kwame Toure and had been married for a time to the famous South African singer and composer Mariam Makeba. For work, he had become an aide to President Sekou Toure.

I had listened to Mariam Makeba's music for years, loved it and was a from-the-distance admirer for her struggle for equality and dignity in then apartheid South Africa. In fact, I had even met her in Bamako where she and her band of Liberian musicians had been for a concert—the only such event we ever attended in Mali. She told the crowd in heavily accented French, "Sorry my French is weak; I was colonized by the English."

One of my black American colleagues had invited her and her band to his house for a post-concert reception in Bamako, for which

Joy and I were included and gladly attended. I introduced myself and said my welcomes and started to tell her how much I admired her music but she quickly looked away and ignored me. We were obviously not going to break down any racial barriers that day, but I loved laughing and talking with her Liberian band members.

To the newcomer or visitor, Conakry looked like a mess where nothing had been maintained or fixed for years, if ever, despite the fact that Guinea was one of the most mineral rich countries anywhere with large deposits of bauxite, iron ore, gold, diamonds and more. Roads had massive potholes, outdoor markets were askance, many shops were closed and abandoned, and there were no modern hotels, though one near the bay was actually under construction. The government ministries I visited for my work were in shambles.

The official name of the country was "The Peoples' Democratic and Revolutionary Republic of Guinea", which had to tell you something. I had one meeting with officials of the Ministry of Agriculture, and passing through the Ministry's central foyer, there was a large six-foot tall pile of documents strewn helter-skelter in the middle covered with a thick many-years layer of dust. These were apparently the Ministry's files.

I was told in advance that members of the Guinea government were supposed to answer the phone, when the phones worked, by saying "Ready for the revolution" in French. That proved to be true except the functionaries I witnessed had shortened it to just "Ready". These must have been the cool guys who knew what was trending.

Guinea was neither democratic, nor to my knowledge particularly revolutionary, but it was a naturally beautiful place outside Conakry and, with Sekou Toure aging and starting to fade from the scene, change or something like it was in the air.

This was the essence of a conversation I had with some Lebanese merchants in their downtown shops. In fact, they reported to me that Toure was apparently ill and had flown to a clinic in Cleveland, Ohio, of all places, for treatment.

Going back to Dakar was like going forward in time and efficiency by decades compared to Conakry or even Banjul. I was coming to really love Dakar, and what was there really not to love? This was not to diminish the severe development issues we confronted at work, but it was a place we could happily balance life and work.

The truth was that Senegal was a popular assignment and country for practically all of my colleagues. We all came to like and admire the culture, the mainly beautiful setting of Dakar and the Senegalese themselves—confident, comfortable in their skins, smart.

In an Africa full of "strongmen" leaders who, once gaining power, often anointed themselves leaders-for-life and had to die to leave office, or be overthrown by the next despot in line, the truth for Senegal was just the opposite. They had never had anything except a peaceful and orderly transfer of power after elections once independence from France was won; that was truly admirable and, at that time, almost unique for Africa.

In fact, Senegal's first president, Leopold Senghor, was a Catholic in a largely Muslim country, a renowned poet, married to a French woman and even a member of the *Academie Francaise*.

When Senghor's second term expired in 1980, power was peacefully transferred to his former Prime Minister, Abdou Diouf. I had briefly met Diouf at the ground-breaking ceremony for the Manantali Dam in Mali the year before.

We had developed a deep affection for Mali and Malians but we soon felt the same way about the Senegalese, though the market vendors could be aggressive and off-putting at first.

All transfers of power in Senegal to this day have been peaceful and with a minimum of rancor—a positive example for the rest of Africa.

Our house on Dakar's Corniche overlooked an ocean-side cliff; the food was wonderful and seafood was even sold door to door; we had a regular beach destination with friends where we could windsurf, sail, or go deep sea fishing.

Great restaurants were nearby with Senegalese, French and even Vietnamese cuisine. The American Club with its tennis courts was five minutes away, and I tried to work on my game when I was not at the office or traveling to Banjul. The Almadies, a point of land jutting westward in the Atlantic, was the closest point to North America in Africa and the site of restaurants featuring kora players and craft markets and was a much visited place on weekends. Years later, a new and grand US Embassy would be built nearby.

Joy and I had also recently added a new family addition, a second daughter who had also been born in Austin. In Dakar, she loved the beach and I would amuse her by playing guitar and singing while she played in the little kiddie pool in our front yard.

Sooner or later, almost every Foreign Service Officer is assigned

(forced) to the care and feeding of CODELs (Congressional Delegations) and their staff to his country. We never had to bother with
them in Mali as it was too far off the beaten path, not to mention hot
and miserable for them to come, but in Dakar, we had them—not
many but enough to get our attention, and for junior officers, to
raise blood pressure over the limits with often wild, unreasonable
and unrealistic demands—sometimes constantly changing—which
we had to try to accommodate.

There was one Republican senator I was to meet post-Dakar who
insisted on a squash match at every stop, with a special brand of
mineral water, Evian, waiting at the end of the match. No matter
that squash wasn't available in most countries. We were supposed
to make it happen.

We had one CODEL from a Pennsylvania, a Democrat Congressman and ex-Protestant minister and his aides for a three-day stay.
We knew he liked to play tennis so we proposed one itinerary with
Senegal Government briefings, a visit to one or two USAID projects,
a visit with Peace Corps volunteers, followed by a tennis match back
in Dakar. Option two was an Embassy briefing, one USAID site visit
and more tennis. It turned out that they wanted an option three: all
tennis, and the Ambassador (a good player) and I (unofficially the
post "Tennis Officer") as doubles opponents.

We played numerous doubles matches—I thought Congressmen
went on these trips to find out the "realities going on in the field" and
not just while their time away playing tennis or the like. No, that would
have been a waste of taxpayer money and a big boondoggle, right?

So we played and we played and we played. When Pan Am's return
flight was delayed a day, we were right back on the court.

I was probably at my tennis best, and the Ambassador was no
slouch either, so against the Congressman and his aide, we never
considered that it was part of the protocol that we should lose in
order to be nice, so we played to win.

At one point the Congressman rushed the net just as I let off a
strong cross court backhand that nailed the Congressman directly in
the chest. He immediately collapsed and for a few seconds didn't move.

Rats, I've just killed a Congressman. Not good for him obviously,
and probably not career enhancing for me.

Finally he started to move and eventually managed to stand up. I
apologized as did the Ambassador, and I breathed a big sigh of relief.

Dakar, fortunately was "CODEL light" but more, many more—

some genuine horror stories—lay ahead.

A New Zealand friend and I started something that my Kiwi buddy had been involved with previously in Singapore, something called the Hash House Harriers.

Hashers' claim to fame was described as being either a running club with a lot of post-run beer drinking or as a drinking club that included running. Either description was accurate. We had also made friends with our British Embassy colleagues, and we tried to be helpful when the Falklands War broke out and Dakar served as a refueling point for British aircraft en route to the conflict zone; next stop after Dakar, Ascension Island in mid-Atlantic.

We also started another tradition, the "Annual Anglo-American Beer Degustation Championship" where we sent out formal invitations and were instructed to show up in "national dress". Given the heat, I took that to mean Bermuda shorts for the Brits and T-shirts and shorts for the Americans. I took my cowboy hat just in case I was underdressed and more authentic wear was needed. Both Ambassadors participated and made hilarious serious-sounding opening speeches, tongues planted firmly in cheek.

The competition was restricted to locally made and available beers: Flag, Cardinal, Gazelle and a couple of others. Well organized and with blind tasting, the first winner was soon crowned-—myself to my surprise. My prize was a rough wooden plaque with an inscription as "Champion, Anglo-American Beer Degustation Championship, Year 1"! The next year I was a miserable failure at defending my crown, but I had shone well at the start. After all, it was all about God and Country.

We were fortunate to have many other non-work distractions in Dakar—beaches, cookouts, windsurfing, a softball team and for me, tennis, excursions to the nearby "Pink Lake" and local Senegalese fishing villages. We also made a weekly habit of meeting for beers at various outdoor bars or restaurants calling ourselves the "Bas Foncionnaires" or "Low Level Bureaucrats" Club. Our French friends of course lectured us on our poor French (done on purpose with tongue in cheek) since the real French translation of "Low Level Bureaucrats" was "Foncionnaires Sub-Alternes", but we didn't care.

More than anything, we came to respect and admire the Senegalese. They were self-assured, mostly hard-working and with a vibrant culture. In my view, the music was especially good, with musicians like Youssou N'Dour, Cheick Lo, Baaba Maal and many more. Their music became popular in the greater world outside Senegal, especially in Europe and even the US.

OMVG work continued, aerial mapping of the river basin was carried out by a US firm and successfully concluded, and the Michigan team expanded their field work and research. We had a terrible *harmattan* period that year, with dust off the Sahara often delaying our aerial mapping team from flying. We prayed for clear weather as the contract required us to pay even for down days when it was too dusty to fly or achieve suitably clear photos.

We also continued to keep our ears on the situation in Guinea. Then one day the news arrived. Sekou Toure, the leader of Guinea since the end of colonialism and independence from France in 1958, had died in Cleveland at a famous heart clinic at the age of sixty-two.

Given Guinea's vast mineral resources, surely there was hope that a more democratic successor to Toure could better help Guinea realize its great potential, but time would tell on that score. In the meantime, Toure would be buried back in Conakry, and some of the leaders of countries friendly to Guinea would attend.

On the US side, Vice President George H.W. Bush was appointed to represent us, though I suspected that he would spend little actual time in Conakry but rather base his coming and going out of Dakar.

Future Secretary of State James Baker, Bush 41's dear friend from Houston, summed up their duties during those days: "You die, we fly."

Such proved to be the case. VP Bush and Barbara Bush soon arrived and met the extended US Embassy staff at the downtown Chancery building. Joy and I gathered round with the rest of the guests and listened to his friendly and low-key remarks, much impressed, and spoke briefly with the VP and Mrs. Bush.

Vice President Bush, who later as President we would just call "Bush 41", and this being the more relaxed pre-9/11 world, was staying the night at the US Ambassador's residence which happened to be adjacent to my own house, around the corner and a bit away from the Corniche. I had heard the VP's itinerary and figured that at one point he would be passing in front of my house en route to the Ambassador's residence to spend the evening, then continuing on to Conakry for a brief funeral stay the next day.

So, my four-year-old first daughter and I walked to the curb of the Corniche outside our residence's wall. I asked our residential guard, Monsieur Sall, to please put away his spear and bow and arrows for the occasion. I had given my daughter a small American flag that she waved until we heard the small roar of a motorcade coming in our direction—three Senegalese police escorts on big motorcycles followed by Bush's black Vice Presidential limousine that had been flown in from DC. I hoisted my daughter onto my shoulders as she continued to wave the flag.

Vice President Bush's limo slowed at the sight, stopped and he lowered the window. "Well, hello," he said. "What's up with you?"

The Vice President was a friend to my Texas family and my father-in-law, who had been active in Texas politics and had helped start VP Bush in Texas politics back when he decided to leave Midland to run for Congress representing a Houston district. I mentioned my father-in-law's name and added that this was his friend's grand-daughter on my shoulders.

"Well, I'll be," said a smiling Vice President Bush in his slightly nasal accent, "it's a small world."

This was a big event for us, as this kind of thing—being around the great and near-great—didn't happen every day. So I thought that the episode was over. The VP's short motorcade continued on to the Ambassador's residence and Bush proceeded on to Conakry the next morning for Toure's funeral, soon returning to DC.

But after Vice President Bush returned to Washington, out of the blue Mrs. Bush called my mother-in-law in Austin. "Just wanted to let you know that we saw your kids in Dakar, and they're fine," she said.

This was not the last time I overlapped with George H.W. Bush, but that story comes later.

———

It was hard to keep up with events from the outside world. It was better than Bamako where we received the *Washington Post* a month late. In Dakar, there actually was TV—one channel in French and Wolof—and we even had a home telephone that was mostly a decoration but occasionally worked for local calls. We were still largely cut off from anything happening at home, except what we heard on the BBC and Armed Forces Radio.

The one exception was that we could buy the Paris-printed Herald Tribune from the day before at street-side kiosks in downtown Dakar. We could keep up with vital information like college basketball scores, and I was aware that my school was making a run well into what would come to be called March Madness. In fact, they made it all the way to the NCAA finals and, we assumed and hoped, we could at least tune in to the game on Armed Forces Radio which we could occasionally pick up on shortwave.

Along with a couple of my colleagues from Indiana—fellow college basketball enthusiasts, to put in mildly—I decided to stay up late to listen to the NCAA finals, which was being broadcast from New Orleans.

The game faded in and out on AFN. My team had the ball and there was about a minute left in the game with the lead going back and forth. Then, suddenly, we lost the signal and I panicked. Thinking of every alternate frequency I could remember, I finally got the signal back. There was just a few seconds remaining in the game when a freshman on our team took the shot. It was good. The broadcaster conveyed that the shot was made by a young fellow with the last name of Jordan.

We had won. I looked over at my Indiana friends, by this time fast asleep on the couch. So, I proceeded to have a single solitary joyous celebration on my street in Dakar. I was no good at work the next day but for once I didn't care. The moon and the stars had aligned and victory, even in West Africa, was sweet. I was one happy Tar Heel.

One more basketball note: One look at the young men of Senegal, many standing well over six and a half feet tall, and it was clear that these guys had the potential to be big-time basketball players. The only things lacking—and these were essential—were decent coaching, a culture that valued the game and certainly more and higher quality facilities where they could practice.

I even met one US college coach, from the University of Maine and ahead of his time, who was in Dakar to scout prospects. He ended up offering one young man (whose mother was a national employee of USAID) a scholarship to play college ball in Maine.

Fast forward to the present: basketball is well established in Senegal and US college coaches and the NBA have long since taken notice. A steady stream of Senegalese players continue to play at the US college level and a few are even in the NBA, like Minnesota's Gorgui Dieng or the Celtic's Tacko Fall.

Back in Banjul, the work of the Michigan team was in full stream.

Once the research behind the environmental, economic and aquatic work was done and reports written, the last step was to be a key synthesis report that would focus future planners on the best course of action for the Gambia River Basin.

In preparation for the final phase of the Gambia basin studies, UM decided to have a preliminary review meeting of results to date back at their home base of Ann Arbor. I was the USAID representative for the meeting and my favorite Senegalese colleague, Mamour Gaye, was chosen to represent OMVG.

We had only one significant issue: the meeting was held in mid-January and it was bitter cold in Michigan. Bad enough for me given my Texas roots, but it was an unspeakable horror for Mamour.

In fact, once we arrived at the hotel, he took me aside and spoke to me with all sincerity. "I'm not leaving the hotel," he said. "I can't, it's too cold."

I went to the meetings for us both and reported to Mamour at the end of the day.

We transited Washington, DC, on the way back to Dakar on the day which happened to be the date of President Reagan's second inauguration. The temperature in DC fell to historic lows—well below zero—and the inauguration was moved inside the Capitol. Mamour once again took refuge in the hotel while I passed time going from movie theatre to movie theatre, waiting impatiently to fly back to the sea breezes and warmth of Senegal.

It was becoming obvious that the conclusions of the OMVG would not amount to a wholesale endorsement of the original development plans including the construction of the impoundment dam at Kekreti and the salt-intrusion dam downriver at Balingho. I think USAID and the Michigan team both had shared a positive and optimistic hope that the ambitious plans could be realized. After all, we were talking about providing greater opportunity through vastly improved agricultural production, and thus incomes for the affected population, but we had to keep an open mind to see what the studies and the science foretold.

I guess it was a little like what Reagan was telling Gorbachev on the entirely different subject of arms control: "Trust but verify," he kept saying, so we decided to wait and see.

However, from our informal conversations with Michigan team members, and then again when we started to see draft reports, it was clear that the results and recommendation were not to be what

OMVG leadership expected, and to a certain degree what USAID had expected either. There were issues across almost every aspect of the planned interventions that would have impact, much of it negative, on the Basin's aquatic and terrestrial ecology, water associated health and most significantly on the potential of rural development based on the two dam scheme and its many associated impacts.

In brief, some of the impacts were judged as being fatal to much of Gambia's mangroves, the engine of the river's fishery and shrimp production; areas of present Gambia's rice production would be lost and the increased production envisaged by developing the dams and new irrigation would take years to realize; Basin states lacked trained personnel to affect increased agricultural production, transport or storage; large resettlement programs of up to 18,000 rural villagers would be required; diseases like schistosomiasis would increase; and internal rates of return for the various dams and irrigated agriculture were more modest than originally expected.

Of course, positive benefits were identified as well, and the final wording of the report would prove to be masterfully diplomatic. But the reality was clear enough: there would be serious negative impacts on the OMVG states if the originally conceived projects were in fact developed.

More to the point, with the publication of the reports and their wide dissemination to the donor community, it would be difficult to see how scarce development funds would be dedicated by donors to projects that could actually cause harm.

Rule number one of development, as in medicine, was simple: do no harm.

———————————

Other moments of two tours in Senegal still stand out vividly in my memory: our house shaking as the supersonic Concorde made its final approach into Yoff airport; going deep sea fishing for sailfish off the coast; learning how to play boule with French friends; listening to Kora players at restaurants at the Pointe des Almadies; Monsieur Sall accompanying us to the airport for our wee hours Pan Am flight and saving our place in line with his spear at the ready; putting my wife and little girls on the Pan Am flight to New York and vividly recalling the 747's name emblazoned on the its nose—"Maid of the Seas"—that would later be blown up over Lockerbie, Scotland; befriending Peace Corps volunteers and NGO workers and listening to their tales of working in rural Senegal, and much more.

Career wise, I could hang on in Dakar and continue a very pleasant life until the very end of my second tour, or I could look for my next professional challenge. As it turned out, my next trip to Washington helped me figure it out. Walking the halls of the State Department, I ran into a colleague and friend who asked me what I was going to do next since I was essentially finished in Dakar. When my answer proved to be less than definitive, he walked me into the office of a senior USAID official who was in charge of project development for the Latin America bureau. She was very professional and to the point: "We've checked you out and we have a position in the Costa Rica mission that might be just right for you. Are you interested?"

Costa Rica

LATIN AMERICA HAD BEEN largely off my previous radar screen. I had visited the Mexican-Texas border town of Nuevo Laredo often enough but had only once ventured into Mexico proper. I had never studied Spanish, and the thought of an assignment in Latin America did not initially excite me.

True, it was closer to home; the development challenges would be different than they were in Africa, although still important, and it would certainly be interesting to learn about another culture and possibly learn another language.

Still, going to Costa Rica sounded attractive. I had heard that it was a beautiful place with abundant rain forests, beaches—both Caribbean and Pacific—wildlife, and likely better living conditions when compared to West Africa. But other than that it was a blank in my knowledge.

To qualify for the assignment I had to learn passable Spanish, as would be taught and tested by the Foreign Service Institute in northern Virginia near DC. I had done well in language classes previously, although speaking was a different story, I had learned, than textbook language studies. Nevertheless, I earned my required level within nine weeks.

On our first LASCA flight to our new home in San José, I sat beside a gentleman who would become a harbinger of my future environment—a Nicaraguan sympathizer of the "Contras"—the anti-communists who were confronting the leftists (or, as some would say, the *Sandanistas*) in neighboring Nicaragua.

He was friendly and also the first recipient of my newly-minted and surely painful-sounding Spanish. As in France years before, I was understood but it hardly amounted to fluency. To say the least, my Spanish needed work.

Our flight landed after descending over green forested mountains and we were met by representatives of my new office (already an improvement over Mali where we had not been met upon arrival at all) and were soon deposited in a semi-modern villa in a San José suburb. There was even a separate play area for the kids. So far, great!

I had been warned that instead of the polo shirt and sandals dress of Mali, or the khakis and dress shirt attire of Senegal, my colleagues in Costa Rica wore coats and ties to work every day. And socks, too!

In Mali, we'd joked that we'd had to wear socks exactly twice a year—at the Fourth of July reception and at the Marine Ball each November eleventh. So, in Costa Rica this would be an adjustment, but only a minor one; I had not forgotten how to tie a Windsor knot despite my recent lack of practice.

My new US and Costa Rican colleagues were an impressive bunch and the work was very different from my recent West Africa routine. We were all about helping Costa Rica make fundamental economic reform—changing from a statist and protectionist economy to a more open, export oriented nation. This required policy reform by the Ticos, which, as they acknowledged, was long overdue, as well as a new emphasis on export promotion of products such as livestock, cut flowers, and other agricultural products.

It also entailed promotion of quality foreign investment into new industries such as high-tech IT, agriculture and textiles, as well as the tourism sector, the latter (at the time) being nascent as compared to the economic dynamo that it would eventually become.

With Costa Rica's rich and abundant natural resources, we wanted to help the Costa Ricans promote these attractions while protecting their amazing rainforests, national parks, beaches, aquatic resources and agricultural lands from over-exploitation. Costa Rica was a verdant jewel and it needed to be preserved as one, all while promoting growth and investment.

I was beginning to see the beginnings of a win-win-win with our development and reform program: we had support and money from the US Government; a willing and reform-minded host country in Costa Rica, and a qualified and hardworking USAID staff, the great majority of whom were Costa Ricans. Surely a formula for success, but it was also clear that we had a long way to go. If we did our job correctly, we had the possibility of helping our Costa Rican colleagues transform an entire economy—one that if reformed positively, could create jobs, opportunity and better conditions for a majority of Costa Rica's citizens.

To me, this was enough to motivate me to apply my knowledge and skills to this endeavor so, along with my impressive USAID colleagues and the just-as-impressive Costa Rican colleagues with whom I was now working, we could make a positive difference.

The President of the Central Bank knew exactly the reforms that needed to be undertaken, and he welcomed our help. And our financing! I had heard that he had graduated from university in Geneva and spoke French. I was mightily tempted to switch back to French but stuck as best I could with Spanish.

I also met the Costa Rican Vice President, Jorge Manuel Dengo, who was altogether impressive, welcoming and kind. What good people with whom to work!

I admit that the Costa Rican Spanish was not the Spanish I had supposedly learned at FSI. It seemed they would "*vosotros*" each other and the dog, yet "*tu*" the president. And what the heck was this "*vos*" they kept using? *That* had not been mentioned at FSI!

I knew my language skills would improve, but I still missed the easy fluency I had speaking French. That said, there were so many fewer social and economic impediments to befriending the locals. This often started with a Tica that knew some English, or had a tie to the US—a common occurrence—and then branched out from there. Soon we had a nice and growing circle of Costa Rican friends, as well as others of various nationalities, especially Dutch (for some reason), who we would value for the duration.

Soon I was playing tennis, squash and golf with new friends, and we were often invited out. The work was very demanding, and we worked long hours, but we were dedicated to it while at the same time we tried to maintain balanced lives. (After all, we had two active volcanoes to see not far away, rain and cloud forests a couple hours' drive from our base, the Pacific beaches over the hills of the Meseta Central, raging white-water rivers on all sides, incredibly good fishing on both coasts and on many rivers, and much more!) While we'd had had no idea what we were getting into when I was first assigned, Joy and I had to agree that this little country was drop-dead gorgeous.

Workwise, this was my first exposure to a balance-of-payment reform program that the USG would establish for truly friendly nations who were in financial dire straits and willing to institute reforms. We would negotiate a list of economic reform measures that the country needed to undertake, and in return provide them a package of support funds that they would use to pay off external debt to institutions like the IMF or World Bank. This promoted both reform and stability.

It became clear early in our assignment that the Contra-Sandanista conflict to the north of us was something that would significantly affect Costa Rica. Central America was a small bridge of land, and Nicaraguan refugees were an increasing presence on the Costa Rica border and within the country. A hospital for wounded Contras was operating in San José, and the US Embassy worked to protect both our staff and help preserve Costa Rica's stability.

Costa Rica had not had a military since 1948, and they were proud of that tradition. Although they had a police force, it wasn't quite the same thing, so we worried a bit for our safety if the rebels decided to make trouble. Costa Ricans liked to say that they had decided to devote funds that had once been for the army to other uses, like education and health care, and in that regard they were certainly ahead of their time, but that laudable policy did not necessarily translate into tranquility across the border to the north.

The Sandanista-Contra conflict brought us more than our fair share of CODELs (Congressional Delegations) and STAFFDELs (Congressional Staff Delegations) that we constantly were expected to brief, accompany to meetings with host government officials, or onsite visits outside the capital.

I had noted that the climate in Costa Rica was warm and wonderful when Washington, DC, was snowy and freezing, and for some reason we seemed to get a lot of CODELs during the DC winter, but I am sure that was just a coincidence....

There may have been some low-level grumbling about these expected duties, and sometimes a constant stream of visitors could slow down the other work, but we understood that it was important or even vital for members of Congress to know what we were doing, to understand it and, if they were so inclined, to support us.

Costa Rica was seen as an island of stability and cooperation in a turbulent region—and our Embassy work was contributing to US policy—and I supposed it didn't hurt for our visitors to exit a cold and snowy DC to take temporary refuge with us in Costa Rica.

We welcomed many of the well-known Congress people of the day—my own congressman from Austin, Jake Pickle, had been a protegé of LBJ and was a heavy hitter. The venerable senator and former Governor from North Carolina, Terry Sanford, was building schools when other Southern Governors were blocking them, and he had always been one of my heroes. More than once we received a personable congressman from Harlem, Charles Rangel, and he seemed engaged and interested. Our paths would cross a few times later in other areas of the world.

Our USAID balance of payments program was reserved for close ally countries needing special economic support. We would first negotiate a series of needed economic policy reforms with the Central Bank and Ministry of Finance, and then the Government of Costa Rica could use the foreign exchange to international debtors like the IMF, World Bank or even the USG, promoting economic stability while drawing down essential debt.

Taking part in these negotiations, I was able to renew my knowledge of economics while in the meantime dealing with the country's impressive and personable Vice President, Minister of Finance and Central Bank President.

The balance of payments program had one unique aspect. For every dollar provided under the program, we required the Costa Ricans to make a dollar equivalent in local currency available to be deposited in a separate account and then programmed by the two governments for additional development activities that would complement the regular US dollar program.

After several years, the local currency fund totaled in excess of $1.0 billion. There was just one minor detail associated with that fund that was not clearly agreed upon by the Americans and the Ticos—the ownership of the money! Just whose money was it, anyway?

We freely admitted that the money could not be ours as Congress had not appropriated it, so in our view the funds indisputably belonged to Costa Rica.

The Costa Rican government's lawyers and other officials were shocked by the news as they had a similar issue—the equivalent of the Costa Rican congress had not approved it either, so it couldn't be theirs.

So the strange and unique kabuki dance of two sovereign governments basically saying about the money: "It's yours", "No, it's yours", "No, yours", persisted for months until the fertile legal minds of our Tico counterparts figured out a way of making what was not "theirs" at least "theirs enough" to keep us all out of trouble.

That accomplished, we proceeded to mutually program a significant and an additional developmental resource for the country. Of this group of Costa Rican colleagues, one was to be a future Vice President and another a future President of the Republic—both women.

The local English language newspaper, *The Tico Times*, accused us of operating a "parallel state" with the local currency, whatever that meant. So, in my job description it should have read under the "Duties" section, "Manages the parallel state", I suppose.

We eventually stopped requiring that local currency be made available—the amount was becoming too staggering—and we started to have worries about inflationary impact of the funds. So, with the Costa Ricans' full approval, we agreed to endow local schools, business and agricultural universities and other institutions with *"fedicomisos"*—trust funds—that to this day have operated for their sustainability with far fewer financial limitations than would otherwise have been the case.

In Costa Rica, paradise was close enough to see and touch and it would have been criminal not to have taken advantage of the many opportunities. We soon visited the smoking volcano at Arenal and spent a couple of days hiking with friends around the Cloud Forest of Monteverde. It was the rainy season, and during the rainy season in Costa Rica, unlike the rainy season in Mali which meant it could rain in theory but rarely did, it rained and rained and often rained for long hours in torrents.

It was a fine relaxing sensation to listen to the rain pound of your rooftop during evenings, but when you had to be out and about, raingear, umbrellas and hats were necessary.

It almost never stopped raining our entire stay at Monteverde, but our hikes and persistence were rewarded with sightings of the quetzal with its red breast, resplendent long green tail and its booming deep click of a call. Quetzal sightings were rare, our guide told us, even in Monteverde.

Our good fortune held as we even stumbled across a number of bright orange toads amid the thick dripping greenery of the forest. By the time we departed Costa Rica almost five years later, naturalists were telling us that the orange frogs had gone extinct, but he hoped they were wrong and that the little show-offs were just hiding.

There was another variety of frog, however, that we could have managed without—huge green monsters the size of footballs that hung out on our lawn, especially during the pouring rain, looking at me as I tried to open our front gate. Our little girls were frightened

39

of them since the frogs were practically big enough to carry them off.

Family wise, we were fortunate. The girls were happy with their Country Day School, instruction in English, but they were also rapidly picking up Spanish. They flatly refused my efforts to speak to them in French as they told me, "That's not what they speak here, Daddy." Our youngest daughter, then four, loved her Costa Rican pre-school classes and was totally convinced she was Costa Rican, singing away in Spanish for us.

Wife Joy found a job with the Inter-American Institute for Human Rights, which she liked and which kept her busy. The only bad part was when the Institute sent her to Haiti to work during the Haitian elections. Some Haitians waiting in line to vote in Port au Prince were gunned down not far from where she was working, forever making her wary of ever again setting foot in Haiti, a circumstance that would affect us later.

We had also become friends with several of our Costa Rican neighbors including a woman, half American, who worked in marketing for a San José television station. She took one look at our blond, curly-haired daughter and soon our little girl had her own spot blowing out birthday candles for a Kodak commercial.

Joy wasn't spared either. She was soon recognized around town as the "Sardimar Lady" smiling at the camera and then smiling radiantly at a can of tuna.

There were a lot of Americans living in Costa Rica including thousands of "*pensionados*", overseas retirees with a pension as income who had chosen to relocate to Ticolandia, as it was sometimes called.

The pensionados received some special privileges like duty-free entry of a vehicle and appliances, and all in all they seemed a diverse group who were mostly content to be in Costa Rica and to profit from its many attractions and diversions.

One of the long-time San José Americans I met had a small band that played bluegrass, country and old rock 'n roll tunes. Somehow I ended up trying out for the band and was welcomed into it.

I would almost never have considered such a thing in the US as I had doubts about my musical talent compared to incredible musicians everywhere in the US, but in Costa Rica the gringo musical gene pool was much smaller, so I decided to give it a try. I figured the embarrassment would be manageable.

Soon we were playing less bluegrass and more old rock 'n roll and having fun entertaining our friends and strangers alike. Our favorite venue was a classic downtown bar called the Key Largo that was frequented by gringos and locals alike. There always seemed to be a large number of friendly young local lady Ticas who were all dressed up and seemed interested in flirting with everyone male, even the scruffier gringo crowd.

We performed a couple of times a month, me playing guitar and harmonica, but our lives changed when we met Nat.

Nat was from New Jersey, married to a Tica and had applied to work for the US Embassy as a facilities manager (the guys who kept everything in working order). Nat played guitar like a star (he could play "Johnny B. Goode" better than the Chuck Berry original). He had played with some well-known bands in the US until ending up in Costa Rica.

When Nat joined the band, we put away the bluegrass and country and started playing rock 'n roll. We were the only gringo band in the country so we actually had devoted fans who attended all our gigs. I switched mostly to sax and harps and soon we had a set-up that lasted until the end of my two plus tours there.

As my spouse would so eloquently say, "Playing in a band is cheaper than seeing a shrink."

———

Back at work, the local currency we had accumulated had an added benefit in addition to all the trust funds ("*fedicimisos*") we were setting up. A new and larger US Embassy was being built in a San José suburb that would have been far more secure that the old-time, on-the-street, downtown Embassy which we inhabited then. The old location would have given current Security Officers nightmares, and it was definitely time to move.

So, move we did, but at the time USAID Missions were not re-quired to be physically co-located with Embassies, so we made plans to build our own new USAID headquarters near the new Embassy. Our headquarters was designed to be an impressive structure that could hold our growing mission numbers.

The new HQ was almost embarrassingly nice, but the best mit-igating factor was, I think, it didn't cost the US taxpayer a cent. It was financed entirely with local currency.

Our Costa Rican counterparts seemed to have no issue with the building since it ultimately belonged to them. We figured that one day, if we at USAID were successful with our program, we could depart for good and turn the building over to the government. We knew it would make a good new Central Bank building, or even a new *"Casa Presidentiale"* if that's what they wanted to do with it.

I loved how we hooked the new HQ up to the water supply. Our respected Costa Rican head engineer, Heriberto, knew a Tico water diviner. The diviner came and surveyed the property with his divining rods, and sure enough, an abundant source of water was soon found.

Not long after moving into our new building, I received a call from an American who had lived in Costa Rica for some years and who told me that he was into something he called "eco-tourism" or "adventure travel". Michael's "eco-tourism", which was a new term to me then, was based around white-water rafting. He invited me to participate in an upcoming white-water rafting trip his company was offering. He told me pointedly not to take a day of leave for the trip. "You are working," he told me.

A small group of mostly Americans and Costa Rican guides, plus Michael, met downtown and then proceeded to our jumping off point on the Pacuare River. The expedition would last two days and we would spend the night beside the river and finish after a partial second day of rafting.

Downtown San José could be a little grimy, so we always looked forward to being out in the lush Costa Rican wilderness.

Our guides told us we would travel over eighteen miles of river the first day and traverse some fifty-two sets of rapids. Despite the fact that these were not Class 5 rapids (it is considered unseemly to kill off the tourists and the USAID guy on the first day) it still seemed formidable. We would also be ending the last five miles of day one on some of the best rapids in Costa Rica as we passed through the Pacuare River gorge. We donned our life jackets and helmets, picked up our paddles and after some serious instruction from the guides, we were off.

This was very exhilarating and far better than river rafting that I had done in the US. It was also a beautiful setting we were passing through—virgin tropical rainforests with tropical birds like parrots and toucans overhead. There were even a number of effervescent big blue butterflies winging their way down the gorge as we passed. Wonderful!

Our guides were in-control and never panicked, so the rest of us didn't panic either. And the ride, like the scenery, was first class. We spent the night in tents with cots near the river (it rained, of course) and we finished up the next day at the river town of Siquirres.

Michael had plans to expand his overseas advertising and see if he could tap into a new segment of the as yet underdeveloped tourism sector in Costa Rica. Other entrepreneurs followed up on Michael's lead, and soon thereafter there were additional white-water rafting companies offering river trips all the way up to Class IV rapids. Eco-lodges, rainforest hiking, turtle hatching tours, and zip lines through the jungle would be coming in the near future, and Michael helped to get the ball rolling.

One of USAID's strategy components in Costa Rica was to help the country promote quality exports as well as foreign investment, the whole point being to help generate jobs and economic opportunity.

Tourism, eco-tourism was not the only aspect of this but clearly was and should have been one of the main focuses of this strategy. The beaches were beautiful on both the Pacific and the Caribbean sides, yet the existing infrastructure of hotels, lodges and other accommodations were often too basic and too mediocre to be of much interest to foreigners.

———————

One of the important Costa Rican agencies we supported both from a grant and local currency program was CINDE, the Costa Rican Investment Promotion Agency—a non-governmental, private and non-profit organization that was founded a couple years before our arrival in-country.

One of our best US friends was an advisor for CINDE, and we closely followed its development, strategies, plans and successes. CINDE had been conceived by leaders in Costa Rica's private sector with the strong encouragement of the Mission Director of USAID, my boss. We also provided essential funding for CINDE from the outset.

Costa Rica had been hard-hit a few years earlier by an economic crisis, and USAID was very supportive of out-of-the-box thinking by Costa Rican leaders that led to the founding of CINDE.

One of the realizations going into CINDE's founding was that exports from Costa Rica were not competitive externally and foreign direct investment into the country was very limited. CINDE originally focused on trade and export promotion, non-traditional agricultural production and exports as well as education but over the years had come to focus solely on investment promotion. CINDE even opened offices in New York and Miami and staffed the US offices and the Costa Rican headquarters with bright and capable young Costa Ricans.

CINDE investment promotion was based on a model developed by the Irish Development Agency, Ireland's version of USAID, and CINDE even had an Irish advisor from IDA for a while.

Soon CINDE evolved into one of Latin America's premier investment promotion agencies that many other countries in the region tried to replicate, most notably FIDE in Honduras and FUSADES in El Salvador.

CINDE had the advantage of not being an arm of the Costa Rican government and thus was not restricted to paying government level salaries which would have limited its ability to attract top rung talent.

One of CINDE's first major successes was to convince a major US company to manufacture men's shirts in Costa Rica. That investment alone created over 300 new jobs right from the start and just several years after its founding, some 8,000 new jobs were created in the apparel industry in one year alone. Soon more and more foreign companies were subcontracting with Costa Rican firms providing technology, know-how and opening new export markets.

As time passed, CINDE was able to open higher value production in sectors other than apparel, such as electronics, tourism investment and medical equipment. Intel made a huge investment in Costa Rica a few years into the future, based both on CINDE's track record and the personal intervention of Costa Rica's then president.

USAID admired CINDE and valued its contributions to Costa Rica's emergence from economic crisis into what looked to us like a world class success, the proof being thousands of new jobs created in a quickly evolving and improving national economy.

To me, personally, CINDE was a perfect example of what US assistance could help to achieve—helping smart, capable and hard-working Costa Ricans conceive and implement a groundbreaking and successful program that helped to transform the economy and bring benefits to many.

Some days I just loved going to work.

CINDE had emphasized tourism investment from the start, and that sector was developing right before our eyes in new hotels and lodges, improved roads and bridges, and many new supporting businesses—restaurants, shops, markets, airlines, etc.

Some people would lament that the slow pace of a more traditional, rural and off-the-track Costa Rica was disappearing, but jobs and opportunity were being generated, though most Costa Ricans were determined to zealously protect the environment at the same time.

It was also clear that with a little scratching beneath the new glittery surface, the older and charming Costa Rica was still there, just a little further off the main road than before.

———————

We ended up serving five years in Costa Rica. We mostly loved every second of it. The work was important and timely and I think we did it well, and the infinite outdoor and nature-oriented possibilities were the best we'd ever experienced. We were there so long that both our daughters became convinced that they were Costa Rican. We knew that it would be hard to pull up stakes and leave, because it had been a spectacular experience.

Joy and I must have felt at home too as we had our last child, this time a boy, and for once there was no need to go home to Texas for the birth. Our son, Austin, was born in San José.

So, we now had our own little Tico, and since he was born there, he has automatic Costa Rican citizenship for life and is entitled to carry a Costa Rican passport (if he ever gets around to submitting the paperwork).

We were there over three Costa Rican presidents and administrations and the entire term of the middle one, Oscar Arias. Don Oscar got very involved in the Contra-Sandanista conflict and even won a Nobel Peace Prize for his efforts. It was only much later that he was accused of sexual abuse by multiple women journalists and his reputation diminished.

Arias's modest home was near our office and we occasionally saw him outside working in his yard. Costa Ricans, unlike other nationalities, would not have felt the need to have a Presidential Palace as a residence. In fact, the Ticos would have laughed at the thought, and would not have appreciated such a waste of money.

Arias's term overlapped with a significant event in Costa Rica's history—the anniversary of 100 years of democracy—a timeline not synonymous with other countries in the region and one truly deserving of recognition.

Costa Rica's history was a bit different than that of its neighbors and that had determined its more democratic tendencies in stark contrast to that of its neighbors.

Naturally it had been colonized by the Spanish but the thick rain forests and the lack of gold kept the main Spanish administrators in Guatemala and even the closest bishop was up in Nicaragua. Costa

Ricans, instead of developing grand plantations and haciendas, tended towards small farms with plots of coffee and such. Some called it "the democracy of poverty".

The irony of the Spanish inability to find gold in part because of the thick and abundant forests caused them to miss the real story: the forests *were* the gold!

The indigenous people mostly died off or were killed off instead of remaining in significant numbers as in say Guatemala or Bolivia, the latter a country to be in our future.

So, the poorer Spanish or otherwise European colonialists who managed to end up in Costa Rica developed their own form of government and tradition, that tending towards democracy. Of that the Ticos were justly proud.

Many regional heads of state and their delegations planned to attend the ceremonies associated with the one hundred years of democracy anniversary. Presidents from all over the hemisphere were in attendance; we were represented by the well-traveled George H.W. Bush.

It was now "President Bush", or as he would later be referred to as "George H.W. Bush" or "George the Elder" or by those in the know simply as "Bush 41".

President Bush 41 was no longer on funeral duty which had been in his prior VP job description—the "You die, we fly" days were over. He was president now and he got to attend all those worldly events mostly with the still-living. He also didn't have to eat broccoli.

The event brought about much celebration throughout Costa Rica—marches, flag waving, speeches, school events—and with it some genuine reflection about how fortunate Costa Rica was to be living in peace even in dangerous times.

The peace among the Ticos was especially poignant given the bloodshed in neighboring Nicaragua where the Sandanista-Contra conflict raged, and even occasionally spilled over into Costa Rica's northern zone.

The main event for the VIP outside visitors was an afternoon and evening affair held downtown at the National Theatre, a grand old building with its own grand history.

I, like many of my official colleagues, had been pressed into service, not as participants but to make sure our VIPs were taken care of, that we had the exits and doors secured, and that we knew what to do if the Secret Service had to respond in any way, and finally, how to communicate with our support people scattered from the Embassy to the National Theatre venue.

My specific task was to cover one of the inner doors of the theatre and keep an eye peeled on POTUS and his entourage from DC and recognise any sign of trouble or see to any need.

The Sandanists were represented at the event by Daniel Ortega, dressed in his best Sandanista uniform with a red neckerchief tied around his neck. To me, he looked as if he were attired in a Boy Scout uniform.

The attendees were seated by country delegation. POTUS and the rest of the US delegation were near the front, Ortega and his Sandanista group safely separated from the "*Norte Americanos*" and seated near the middle.

All was proceeding well with me doing door duty until one of the ushers approached me in some haste. He said that the delegation from Uruguay hadn't shown up and there was an embarrassing gap in the appearance of the theatre for television, so he was recruiting the riff-raff, second rung folks like myself, to fill in the empty seats. Suddenly I found myself sitting right beside the Sandanista delegation with Ortega just a couple of rows away.

Maybe it was me but they seemed a pretty grim bunch, and since I then and forever looked like your classic gringo, I hoped that peace and relative harmony would prevail for the duration of the evening.

It did; but the speeches were interminable and it was pushing midnight when our delegation—up since early morning when they had departed DC—finally made for the exits.

Happy at this development, I too made my way up the theater ramp toward the exits. Just then President Menem of Argentina and President Borja of Ecuador appeared to interrupt POTUS as he made his exit.

"Tennis?" he said. "Doubles, first thing in the morning, he and President Borja versus POTUS and Secretary Baker. What do you say?" I think I saw President Bush slightly roll his eyes.

POTUS was as kind and considerate a gentleman in public life as I had ever seen; I never saw a moment of serious irritation in all the times I was around him, but as tired as they were, I doubted that early morning tennis was very high on his "to do" list.

I was right beside POTUS by this time and heard his reply: "Well, we would like to play, but we didn't bring any tennis gear with us." Then he turned to an aide and asked, "I don't suppose we can find some tennis gear for tomorrow at this late hour, could we?" I strongly suspect that he was hoping for a hopeless shrug from the aide.

However, the aide turned to me, knowing I was with the Embassy and said, "What do you think? Is that possible?"

I answered truthfully that I could provide rackets, balls, and all the tennis playing clothes one might need. After all, I had been named "Tennis Officer" in Dakar by my colleagues (as opposed to real functions like "Security Officer" or "Duty Officer") since I usually got the assignment of playing with visiting congressmen and other VIP visitors.

So, it had been my job to be prepared on the tennis front, and I was. The aide escorted me home in one of the Embassy vehicles and I loaded him up with rackets, balls, plus shorts, shirts, shoes and towels.

I made it to the court the next morning in time to see the president and secretary finishing up their second set against Menem and Borja.

I was not surprised at the result. Bush 41 and Secretary Baker were both good athletes and very experienced tennis players (Bush had been an accomplished baseball player in college) and the two of them had been senior doubles champions for several years running in Houston.

They were clearly a few levels above most players their age, but they were also great sports; no disputes broke out, no wars were declared or blood-feuds started, and a good time was had by all!

On the economic front, Costa Rica was coming around. GDP was growing, foreign direct investment was up, tourism from abroad was entering a new and better stage, Costa Rica's image as a peaceful and reforming nation was becoming known abroad.

This was due to several factors, the most important of them being that Costa Rica was led by capable reformers. It didn't hurt either that President Arias had put Costa Rica on the international map with his Peace Prize. And in truth, Costa Rica's donors, led by the United States, were determined to help the national leadership with the support they needed and requested: policy reform ideas, focused technical assistance over key sectors, and enough financial and political support from Washington to make it all come together.

It was a development cliché to say that our assistance was always to help the recipient government to do what they needed and wanted to do anyway. Never was it that we, the foreigners, did this or that, but rather that we assisted the locals to do what they conceived, needed and were determined to carry out themselves.

The reality in some countries wasn't always like that, but in Costa Rica it was the truth. This alone—not to mention the spectacular scenery all around us—made it a very rewarding place to work.

Three more priorities for USAID were emerging: support for improved administration in the justice sector, meaning some reform of legislation governing the sector; training of judges and prosecutors; and helping to make the legal system in general work better and more efficiently.

Secondly, we provided endowments for the establishment of an agricultural college near the city of Guapiles in the tropical zone halfway between San José and Puerto Limon on the Caribbean coast. The name of the school, EARTH, was the most perfect of all made-up acronyms, however in Spanish it was known as the "Agricultural School for the Humid Tropics Region." At its inception, EARTH didn't look like much, surrounded by major agribusinesses especially for export quality pineapples and bananas, but EARTH has survived and prospered and is now a respected regional agricultural institution.

Finally, we decided to get more involved in assisting Costa Rica to protect its national parks and their buffer zones through a variety of interventions that were capably led by Costa Rican environmentalists and politicians. The private sector was largely responsible for growing the burgeoning tourism sector while we helped a variety of public and private institutions protect Costa Rica's abundantly rich and varied environment.

Joy and I were both absorbed with work and our now enlarged family. We knew the work was important, and Costa Rica's progress of reform was taking root all around us in the form of new investment, new jobs created, new economic policies, an increasingly better standard of living, and many more positive changes happening all around us.

We never tired of the spectacular scenery all around: volcanoes and rainforests were not far away. Jungles started not far from the outskirts of San José going east and tree covered mountains going west. Rivers flowed seemingly everywhere—increasingly popular with white water rafters or adventure tourists as they came to be called.

One of my bandmates had a rustic cabin outside the Pacific town of Quepos where we could visit in lieu of our own tropical beach. There we listened to the monkeys yell in the trees above us, and occasionally we could watch sloths slowly make their way down the jungle vegetation toward the beach.

Quepos was also the place where we could do some of the best deep sea fishing in the world. Joy's brother's family came from Texas and together we managed to catch a sailfish or two that, once boated and photographed, we dutifully released into the sea as the law required.

There was no escaping the seasonal rains of Costa Rica either. In Mali or Senegal "rainy season" meant theoretical rain; in Costa Rica, rainy season meant that it would rain in sheets (with an occasional dog or cat thrown in) almost every day between mid-April and mid-September.

There was so much left to see and do in Costa Rica—the list was endless—but we both had that occasionally inconvenient thing called a job that kept our noses firmly to grindstones. That was still a pretty good fate as we were seeing the results of our labors professionally.

Not long after we departed Costa Rica, our Washington bosses had the good sense to declare victory and actually close the office. USAID now has a formal name for this process called the "Road to Self Reliance." However new as that program or slogan was, we always said that if we did our jobs correctly, we were definitely in the business of working our way out of a job.

It actually happened in Costa Rica, and again most of the credit goes to our well-qualified and hard-working Tico colleagues.

With well over two full tours in Costa Rica under our belts, it was time to think about what came next. I was offered positions in Haiti, Jamaica and a few other places, but then I got a call from the USAID Director in Tunisia. It was for the second ranked position in the Tunisian mission, and though by this time I had served occasionally as the acting number two in the Mission, this position would make that promotion official.

It made sense in that I had previously visited and liked Tunisia. USAID had had a well-established presence in Tunisia for years and worked in several key areas such as family planning and health, and it had an international English-speaking school that was fully accredited in the US. With our daughters now old enough for elementary school, this was an important factor.

Leaving was sad. We had to say farewell to many friends. I had to leave a job that was rewarding and colleagues I respected. I had to say goodbye to my band, and also to the golf course five minutes away from my house. Goodbye to wonderful beaches, rain forests and a plethora of tropical wonders.

Yes, I would not miss the neighbor's barking dog that had kept us sleepless on more than a few nights. And I would not miss the strong earthquake tremors that seemed to always hit at about six o'clock on Sunday mornings, prompting us to grab the kids and run outside.

By this time we had traveled all over the country, but I had still to make it to the Panama border on the Caribbean side and down to the Osa Peninsula on the Pacific coast. Much water under the bridge, and much satisfaction, we knew we would find a way to return.

Tunisia

IT TOOK ONLY ONE day for me to lose all credibility with my wife, and I accomplished that immediately upon arrival in Tunis because we arrived in the midst of a major anti-American demonstration.

So much for my assurances that the natives were friendly and welcoming...

It is said that timing is everything, and apparently this timing was pretty terrible. My new soon-to-be major career counselor and influencer, Saddam Hussein, had just invaded Kuwait and the west was starting to organize its response.

The response, of course, was led by President Bush 41, who was aggressively building a strong anti-Saddam coalition of both Arab and Western powers. "This will not stand", the President had stated.

The Tunisians, like almost every Arab country in the region, were apparently pro-Saddam and anti-US. At least that was true for the unruly and angry crowd that greeted us on day one.

I had assured my wife that Tunisia was calm, mostly pro-US, a nice mix of Europe and North Africa, used to and tolerant of western culture, if not exactly welcoming. I think I emphasized its historical ties to France, accessibility to Europe for our next R&R, and wonderful antiquities dating from both Carthage and Rome.

In addition to my credibility problem, it didn't help that our entire family, and our family dog, were confined to a hotel room. Having a house to move into had apparently not been much of a priority to my new office. We were soon to get to know Tunis and its suburbs well as we combed the area searching for quarters.

Credibility: strike two.

On the other hand, the work was interesting. We had some ambitious plans to help Tunisia privatize some very inefficient state-run enterprises to help the country further its export markets by promoting agribusiness—it sure had worked well in Costa Rica—but our living situation was clearly impeding settling into the work.

Our one-year-old son was constantly toddling onto and off marble steps in our temporary house, and his constant bruises made him look like a victim of child abuse. We redoubled our search for housing—at least we were learning our way around town—and we were relieved to finally move into a nice house located near both our office and the Embassy.

We soon found out that one of our neighbors was none other than Yassir Arafat, and that his PLO headquarters was within easy walking distance. He traveled with an entourage everywhere he went, either in his motorcade or crossing the intersection on foot while wearing his obligatory black and white *kaffiyeh*. I assumed that many of the crowd accompanying him were most likely bodyguards and armed to the teeth.

Tunis was interesting enough with both its colonial and Ottoman remains plus a good souk to walk around. Sidi Bou Said, a beach suburb, was lovely.

There was a serene American cemetery from World War II close by where row after row of perfectly placed crosses spread out. The German Afrika Corps had had their way with the green and poorly led Americans in 1942 at the Battle of Kasserine Pass, and the sad results lay before us.

My in-laws from Texas soon came to visit and the cemetery was high on our list of attractions to show them. My father-in-law, a flight surgeon during the war, surveyed the field of crosses and muttered, "There but by the grace of God..."

Also nearby was Carthage, the site of the ancient city rival of Rome founded by the Phoenicians. The Romans destroyed Carthage after Hannibal had earlier created some chaos in Italy that the Romans must not have appreciated. When they sacked Carthage, they went to the trouble of sowing salt into the earth of the ruins. The Romans neither forgave nor forgot.

There was just enough left of the old circular port of Carthage to imagine it in its prime when it had received and launched scores of trading ships from the entire Mediterranean and had made Carthage a thriving hub of commerce.

Ambassador Pelletreau was an experienced and respected Arabist and diplomat, and we were happy to work with him. I enjoyed it when he invited me for tennis at his residence with its clay court overlooking the sea.

Meanwhile we kept a close eye on what was going on in Kuwait. Letters from home were full of fright and worry but in these pre-Internet days, we only had what information we could glean from the BBC or the *Herald Tribune*. We weren't seeing or hearing what the folks at home were hearing.

When I had come to Tunisia back in college days, Tunisia was led by the colonial liberator Habib Bourguiba who was still alive but now aged and infirmed. Bourguiba had been replaced by the more recent one-party strongman ruler, Ben Ali.

Ben Ali would eventually be the first ruler victim of the "Arab Spring" twenty years in the future. As Ambassador, Pelletreau met frequently with Tunisian ruler Ben Ali and would return and brief the staff. Ben Ali's message was that we would be protected and safe, and the current instability would pass and all would return to normal.

My worries didn't get much better when I was dropped off at my house by a local taxi driver. He actually said to me, "Now we know where you live, so we can kill you when the war starts."

I thought about replying, "Then you'll excuse me if I don't tip you."

Our main worry was for our elementary school daughters who took a bus to and from the American School every day. The bus was supposedly supervised by the Embassy and local police, but given the tensions we felt growing, we mainly worried about the kids as did all the other parents.

I decided then to make a purchase I normally would not do. I bought a satellite dish and had it installed at my house. It wasn't long before I understood what had alarmed our friends and family at home.

There was a real and constant drumbeat towards war in the region. It got worse every week and we were finding ourselves right in the middle of what I had to call "hostile territory". This was not looking good.

First the Embassy told us to stock up on food and other essentials in case of an emergency, which we did. Soon we had stockpiled enough food in our pantry to last weeks, if not longer.

We were constantly briefed by Embassy officials and we could not help noticing that, as the days passed and regional tension continued to rise, the official tone from our security people was becoming more and more alarmist, and especially for those families with small children. And there we sat with three of them, our son just having had his first birthday.

The talk was now increasingly about evacuation. How it would work, what to take or leave behind, what help the Embassy could provide. They had our full attention.

In Washington, President Bush gave the Iraqi's a seventy-two-hour ultimatum to either depart Kuwait or face the consequences. A formidable international coalition was now poised in northeastern Saudi Arabia and increasingly ready to react militarily against the Iraqi forces in Kuwait.

The tension mounted for us as we heard about an upcoming and critical meeting planned for that day in Geneva between Secretary of State Baker and his Iraqi counterpart, Tarik Aziz.

I invited my work colleagues to watch the news at my residence via my newly installed satellite dish and some twenty or so of them crowded into my small den.

The talks went longer than expected and our expectation or hope was that maybe that meant some progress was being made. Finally, Secretary Baker came out from the meeting and faced the press. We waited and watched anxiously.

The Secretary said, "We've been meeting for over four hours with Foreign Minister Aziz. Unfortunately..."

There was a collective gasp from my gathered colleagues. We didn't hear what else Secretary Baker said but when we heard the word "Unfortunately" we knew what it meant. It meant inevitable war in the Gulf and a very likely evacuation for all but the most critical staff from the Embassy.

Families like ours with children would certainly be included. Everyone filed out of my den without another word being said and went home to pack a suitcase. Two days later we were gone, never to return.

We left what we hoped would eventually be airfreight on the dining room table. Everything else we just left and hoped that we would see it again someday. We left the car in the garage, never to be seen again and eventually sold by a friend. We hugged the maid and left for good.

Somehow I had a deep feeling of personal failure. The coming Gulf War was not my fault but this—an evacuation after being in-country after only six months—was not how our stay in Tunisia was supposed to end.

Years later I would return to Tunisia as an official US election observer for Tunisia's first free and democratic Presidential election that had been the culmination of the only successful "Arab Spring" uprising. It had taken over two decades for me to finally feel a sense of satisfaction and fulfillment about our stay, however short, in Tunisia.

In spite of the rough beginning there, the grit and determination of the good people of Tunisia had finally made the story—at least the latest installment of it—a hopefully lasting success.

On the first leg of our evacuation home, we flew from Tunis to Paris and then boarded an American Airlines flight bound, for some reason, to Raleigh-Durham. The pilot said something nice about the US diplomats and families on the flight and once we landed at RDU, the family then split up, everyone heading home to Texas except for me who was destined for Washington.

A few nights later, sitting with a friend in a Georgetown bar, we watched the war begin on TV with "bombs over Baghdad". As I watched the incredible scene unfold live and in real time, I wondered to myself, "Now what?"

I knew my family would be fine, safe and taken care of by extended family members and friends in Texas. Me? I decided I would volunteer for every short-term assignment overseas I could in order to fill the time with something hopefully valuable.

First stop, Prague, then the capital of Czechoslovakia before the "velvet divorce" with Slovakia. Our team went in the wake of communism's last gasp to negotiate a balance of payments agreement with the government—a first—and provide some extra landing support as they moved toward open markets. Churches were open again, beautiful castles on the hills, people seemed happy but the vestiges of communism were still evident—Russian cars, no crowds in the streets, shops with little to sell.

The US Ambassador was Shirley Temple Black and she invited us to dinner at her residence. After dinner she graciously showed us around the residence and in the study pulled down her Oscar for one of her films. I remember her hands were like sandpaper when we shook.

Last stop was Budapest, beautiful despite the vestiges of communism, on the Danube. We did our negotiations with the new and willing government of Hungary and saw communism come to an end. Again, churches were open, and people were in the streets and looked happy and free. Freedom looked good and felt good. I turned forty on that trip, and my colleagues toasted me over dinner.

I came back to DC and the Europe Bureau put me to work writing a study to evaluate how the relatively new support program for Eastern European countries was going. I interviewed scores of people, took lots of notes and soon began writing my report. When the report came out, Bureau management was not particularly pleased about the frankness of some of my findings and recommendations. The report made its way to Capitol Hill where it was read by one of the Agency's main Congressional supporters—Congressman David Obey from Wisconsin—one that everyone in the Agency respected. Apparently, he liked the report and began to publicly praise it and thanked the Bureau for having been so forthright and honest in its findings and recommendations.

Suddenly I went from being probable bureaucratic road-kill to being somewhat of a hero. The next thing I knew, I was in the presence of the head of the Bureau. She asked me a starting question: "How would you like to be named the first USAID Mission Director in Bulgaria?"

What a shock, and an honor. I needed an ongoing assignment and being a Mission Director was my Agency's version of a top job and the normal highest aspiration of a USAID FSO.

I started to research Bulgaria and called my wife in Texas with the news. "How would we like to be assigned to Sofia, Bulgaria?" I asked her. She responded with a question: "What do they speak in Bulgaria?" Answer: "They speak Bulgarian." My wife: "Well, I'm not learning Bul—flipping—garian!" "Flipping" wasn't exactly the word she used.

So that was that. Actually, there was no international school there at the time, so we had to eliminate it from consideration. But I would always remember my wife's pithy response, and to quote a Ry Cooder song from that era, "That's the way the girls are from Texas."

Bolivia

THE AIRPORT THAT SERVES La Paz, Bolivia, is on the Altiplano at over 13,000 feet. Our American Airlines flight from Miami landed and we stumbled outside with our luggage in the early morning light and cold thin air surrounded by snow-covered Andean peaks. Our son celebrated our arrival in our new country by throwing up on the sidewalk. This was no reflection on Bolivia, rather the effects of a sudden exposure to high altitude.

I could tell that we were not in Kansas anymore—or any other place I had previously known. If this was not the end of the Western Hemisphere, then it was certainly near it. We came to joke later than the flights into the El Alto airport didn't even have to "start their descent"; they just lowered the wheels and landed.

The common local remedy for altitude sickness was to drink coca tea—the tea that used coca leaves instead of real tea leaves to make a supposed altitude treatment. Trouble was, at least for me, the "maté de coca" tasted terrible and the DEA had classified it as a Class 5 narcotic. We decided to adapt to the altitude as most people did—gradually and by living in it.

La Paz, the capital of Bolivia, was the highest capital city on earth at 11,500 feet but that, however ridiculously high, was still considerably lower than the airport. On the way "down the hill"—as we came to call it eventually—to La Paz itself, we wound down two thousand feet past the huge indigenous city of El Alto, eventually reaching the comparatively more manageable altitude of La Paz.

The "indigenous city" reference meant that El Alto, and in fact the majority population of Bolivia as a whole, comprised some sixty percent of the population—Amara and Quechwa natives. The indigenous peoples were the majority of the population—a unique circumstance compared with the rest of the hemisphere—and though many mixed race people had risen to positions of prominence, the

European-descended population tended to dominate both the business and government sectors. That balance would shift later, but that was the way it was and had been following the arrival of the Spanish.

We were struck particularly by the appearance of the indigenous women. They wore bowler hats, long pigtails for hairstyles and, so we were told, multiple layers of thick petticoats as both the local fashion and probably to ward of the cold of the high plains. The entire group also tended to be thick in their torsos (I assumed from decades of living at high altitude and the task of getting sufficient oxygen to survive). They were an interesting and unique indigenous culture.

I had actually been to La Paz some six months previously as part of my "volunteer for any assignment as long as it's not in Washington" initiative following our evacuation from Tunisia and my temporary duty assignment in DC. The task had been to take part in a "Mission Management Assessment" of USAID there in La Paz. The Director and the Deputy Director definitely did not see eye to eye on much of anything, and the subsequent fallout had thrown the entire operation into disarray. I had joined a team of experienced USAID notables—myself clearly not yet in that category—to investigate and make recommendations for a resolution. Our team was led by a high level USAID woman professional and "Latin America expert", later to become a trusted friend and colleague.

Like my son's arrival at the airport months later, Janet also succumbed to the effects of the altitude. We were talking as we exited the plane and descended the ramp into the airport but then she suddenly went silent. I turned to find her passed out of the ramp. We helped her to her feet, and she was immediately greeted by our welcoming committee from the Mission who sat her down, summoned a bottle of oxygen and began to pour "maté de coca" down her throat. To heck with this Class 5 narcotic stuff! We all loaded into the Mission vehicles and beat feet down the hill to our hotel located in a central plaza of colonial-looking La Paz, 3,000 feet below the airport. When we checked on a woozy but improving Janet a bit later, she recounted what had happened when she had fallen semi-life-like onto her bed.

Vespers and music from a nearby Sunday afternoon church service had drifted over the semi-comatose Janet as she jolted awake. "Oh crap, I'm dead!" she had told herself, thinking that she had entered into the heavenly domains rather than the much more mundane reality where she rested. She had survived, however, and we got to work.

The end result was that after two weeks of detailed interviews with staff, and evaluation of internal operations, as well as the progress of some projects outside La Paz, we concluded that the Mission was indeed truly dysfunctional in just about every way possible. US staff apparently had ongoing bets of which Mission leader—either the Director or Deputy Director—would be removed. We surprised them. We recommended that both be removed, and they soon were.

I had liked the challenge of the work and had been fascinated by my first exposure to Bolivia. What a place! But without any intention whatsoever, the assessment results soon affected me, too. My old boss and Director from Costa Rica replaced the Director, and he wanted me to come with him. I would no longer be Mission management, but we agreed that once the Deputy Director departed, perhaps it could be arranged that I would replace him in that position.

That was enough for me, and my wife agreed. The family was reunited, the USAID program was interesting and valued by the Bolivian authorities, the country was diverse and fascinating, the work important (that story later) and the icing on the cake was that there was an American school for the kids. The lack of a US-accredited school in so many overseas posts often made assignments for families with kids impossible. So, for us, given that we were expected to serve a minimum of two two-year tours at a post, this was "problem solved", at least for the present.

I had made one pleasant friend in my pre-La Paz days in Washington. I met Peter, a USAID newbie, and had liked him from the start. I asked him if by chance he was a softball player, as I had heard that the Mission in Bolivia had a team. He replied in the affirmative. For some reason, I pressed my luck and asked him a second question: "Do you happen to play lead guitar?" To my shock and pleasure the answer again was yes.

That weekend we went to a suburban DC music store and purchased most of what we would need for a band—amps, speakers, microphones, cables and so forth—and in my case a lovely tenor sax and a beautiful white Fender guitar. We were set, and though we were a long ways from actually being musical, it was a start.

My initial work in Bolivia in some ways resembled our work in Costa Rica; we had a Balance of Payments program with economic reform policies to negotiate with the government; we had a robust health and family planning program; a program to help the Bolivians improve and modernize the administration of their justice system; other diverse projects to design and approve. We had a huge PL-

480 food program to manage and a host of other developmental challenges that came with trying to implement a large economic development program in a vast and diverse country that was the second poorest country in the hemisphere after Haiti.

Our work in Bolivia had the constant backdrop of the "drug war". Bolivia, Peru, and of course Colombia, were the source countries of coca cultivation, the primary raw ingredient in the production of cocaine. Bolivia mostly grew the coca leaves and processed it into paste and then shipped most of it to Colombia for its final transformation into cocaine.

While DEA worked on the more hard-core intervention side, USAID's part of the drug war was to try to offer economically viable agricultural alternatives to poor Bolivian *campesinos*.

As usual, it was complicated. Coca cultivation was legal in certain areas of Bolivia, as much of the indigenous population chewed it for either its mild narcotic effect that supposedly numbed hunger and countered altitude sickness. Whatever the use, it was part of the local culture and had been forever and therefore not a simple proposition to eradicate it.

The chosen strategy worked out with the government was to tolerate cultivation for traditional use, but to outlaw and eradicate it for export, and to offer help on growing and marketing alternative crops to help replace lost income from prior coca cultivation and sales.

At the start, I asked myself how we could realistically think that *campesinos* would make enough money growing alternate crops— tropical fruit and spices like passion fruit, pineapples, black pepper, star fruit, hearts of palm and so forth—to realistically compete with the high price of coca.

I soon learned the answer: *campesinos* were at the low end of the coca money chain. The real money was made higher up on the processing and refining line. After some convincing, many of the coca farmers were open to considering new crops if there was money to be made and law enforcement would leave them alone.

The head of the coca growers union in La Paz was a rabble rouser anti-eradication radical named Evo Morales. He didn't cause us much trouble at the time but years later became the first indigenous President of Bolivia. The expulsion of DEA, and ultimately USAID, from Bolivia was the end result, but the point then was to provide farmers enough encouragement, plant material, technical assistance, credit and markets for them to succeed with alternate crops. It was not at all as far-fetched as it had first sounded.

The coca growing zone, or "alternative development zone" where we primarily worked was the Chapare—in a tropical zone "down the mountain" from Cochabamba in the direction of Bolivia's second city, Santa Cruz de la Sierra.

During my first trip to the Chapare, we were told the drug barons had put a price in our heads, but we were protected by the local authorities and made it out with no harm done. As time passed, the government tried to exert more control over the zone, and it felt less and less like a war.

The bad drug guys were still there but seemed to have moved deeper into the Chapare jungle or moved out of Bolivia altogether, relocating their operations further north to the wild-west narco-zones of Colombia.

While the DEA was the more militarized part of the "drug war", we actually managed to do our part, either by chance or with purpose.

The dirt roads that crisscrossed the Chapare rarely had long straight stretches, but those that did often became runways for small "narco-planes", single engine aircraft that would land, pick up coca paste from jungle labs and then be off. That was until someone on our team had the bright idea of building concrete "bus stops" midway on the straight sections. The fact that no buses operated in the Chapare was considered a minor detail.

Anyway, our bus stops took out a few aircraft—they are hard to fly when the wings have been knocked off—and soon we were joking with our DEA colleagues: USAID 2, DEA 0. I visited a couple of the wrecks that were soon pulled off into the jungle, so I knew that the stories were true.

The Chapare was also part of the extended Amazon basin with many huge riverine tributaries, eventually flowing into rivers that flowed into the Amazon much further downstream. We occasionally used Bolivian Navy riverine craft to move around the zone—an experience that revealed another otherworldly face of Bolivia: anacondas hanging in the trees, pink freshwater dolphins in the rivers, and far flung settlements where occasionally tribesmen with little or no prior contact with civilization—especially our kind of civilization—would wander in from the jungle dressing in only a loincloth and carrying a long bow and arrows which they used to shoot fish in the rivers.

There was one more anecdote about the Bolivian Navy, a totally landlocked country save for the extensive Amazonian river complex,

Bolivia having lost its last port and territory on the Pacific in a war with Chile in the late nineteenth century.

The joke was that the admiral of the Bolivia Navy was attending an official reception in Buenas Aires, Argentina, and when introduced in the receiving line, had provoked some laughter and eye-rolls ("Bolivian Navy....?")

The Admiral supposedly replied, "If Argentina can have a Minister of Justice, Bolivia can have an Admiral."

There was at least one controversial aspect of the "Drug War" in Bolivia in that the US actually paid the government for the eradication of a large number of hectares of cultivated coca in zones like the Chapare where such cultivation was illegal. That was a yearly negotiation and some of us front-line guys wondered—sometimes to ourselves—just how sustainable such a policy actually was.

We even penned a Christmas carol about it, tongues totally in cheek, to the tune of Deck the Halls:

> "Deck the Halls with Boughs of Coca, (Fa La La La La, La, La La La)
> Masticate it in your boca, (Fa La La La La, La La La La)
> Trample it in your piscina .....
> 'Til it turns to Cocaina" ...

Maybe you had to be there, but humor was always a good thing. I guess.

The altitude of La Paz, the altiplano and other Andean parts of the country seemed to be an unavoidable presence. There was no predicting how it was going to work on individuals—sometimes a fit US Marine guard from the Embassy who could otherwise jog to the moon and back would be laid up while a heavy smoker would have few problems. Stairs were an issue for most.

Sometimes visitors from the States would have to receive oxygen upon arrival at the 13,500 foot altitude airport, and a few visitors almost died from oxygen depletion.

The "rich" people of La Paz lived as low as possible, at about 9,500 feet, and the center city of La Paz itself was at 10,500 feet—still not for the faint of heart. The poor, the indigenous majority, often lived at the highest possible altitude—the city of El Alto on the edge of the drop-off into La Paz.

In and around La Paz lay the "world's highest everything"—you name it—a ski resort of sorts (a treacherous slope reserved only for crazy people with a strong death wish), tennis courts, squash court and my personal favorite, the "world's highest golf course".

The altitude made the ball do odd things, like a putt being able to travel a couple of hundred meters on the ground given the thin air. To play tennis, as was my habit then, one had to puncture the tennis balls with a pin in order to reduce the air pressure. Otherwise a miss-hit ball would go into low-earth orbit. The golf course was a beautiful one though, and I swear there was a small army of derby-clad "*Cholitas*" grooming the course and the greens daily—down to using scissors to manicure them.

As a family, we were happy. Joy had her favorite job ever, managing an export promotion project with some of the same expats she had worked with in Costa Rica and with a Bolivian counterpart organization that was doing good work and valued her contributions.

Both daughters were enjoying the American school—most of the students were Bolivians—and we hoped that the level of education would keep them up with their peers back in the US. Our young son was in kindergarten and having a great time. We had contracted a trusted local taxi driver to take him to and from school, so every morning he would soon announce, "My taxi's here!!"

At work we were always aware that we had a serious job to do in the hemisphere's second-poorest country, but we were aided by a good and dedicated local staff, mostly serious and competent Bolivian counterparts in the government, impressive private sector colleagues, and always challenging work.

After two years in my first interim position, I moved up to Deputy Director once the incumbent departed, just as I had hoped. I had the same wonderful boss I had had for the latter part of our stay in Costa Rica, so work-wise all was good.

We even moved into a new office building—again mostly funded by local currency—that was a few minutes from our house.

About that time we were also firmly established with this new innovation called email, and for better or worse, our professional lives were never the same again. And to think that we used to depend back in the Mali days on cables to communicate. The communication Stone Age was over but the coming days of addictive zombie-like staring into a iPhone screen was still comfortably well off in the future.

Bolivia's immense geographical and cultural diversity—Andes mountains, altiplano, huge jungle swaths, fertile valleys, Amazon basin rivers, Lake Titicaca at such an altitude it was head to breathe,

Potosi silver mines, the ancient ruins of Tiahuanacu, wine making regions of Tarija, vast agricultural plains around Santa Cruz, the Pantenal wetlands near Brazil, reed boats on Lake Titicaca—continued to amaze.

In the course of my work travels in Bolivia, I even made it a few kilometers from the town where Argentine doctor turned Cuban revolutionary Ernesto "Che" Guevara met his untimely end, as well as the small town in the Bolivian Chaco near Paraguay where supposedly Butch Cassidy and the Sundance Kid met their own fiery demise. Some disagree with that assessment saying that ol' Butch actually survived that 1908 shootout and somehow managed to live out his days in Washington State incognito with his old girlfriend at his side.

There was one more ex-Bolivian whose path was a little warmer than the Butch and Sundance one—Klaus Barbie, the WWII SS "Butcher of Lyon". We had some of the same La Paz café and restaurant haunts as Klaus, who was tracked down with the help of one of our Bolivian-American friends and was finally apprehended from Bolivia and extradited back to Lyon, France, in 1983.

As in Costa Rica, one of my favorite non-work distractions was to play in a mostly gringo rock 'n roll band—seven members, including two female singers, a Puerto Rican keyboard player, a drummer who was a teacher at the school with a Costa Rica "Latin-drummer" as backup, my friend Peter as lead guitar—I had interviewed him for entry into USAID some ten years back (I swear music had nothing to do with his selection)—and myself alternating between back-up electric guitar, saxophone and harps. Our sole Bolivian member was William on bass guitar, who was given all the money we earned from paying gigs. We knew William would miss us when it was all over.

We were called "*Sopa de Pato*" or "Duck Soup" in English, a name I had stolen from a band in Austin. Duck Soup had some glorious moments as we toured the country for an Embassy-related function, playing in Cochabamba, La Paz, Tarija and Santa Cruz. We had "Duck Soup: World Tour of Bolivia" T-Shirts made for the occasion. I guess we had a pretty decent following at our venues, mostly uptown bars, and even Joy told me that we never embarrassed her.

I could not use my official car and driver for *Sopa de Pato* gigs as these were usually emphatically not "official business", so I would call a taxi and pile my instruments, amps, mic stands and miscellaneous equipment into the trunk. I once noticed my driver staring at me via his rearview mirror. After a moment he spoke, saying "I know you." I figured that since being head of USAID/Bolivia was a fairly public position with a lot of televised events and speeches, that that must have been it. But no, he then said "Aren't you the sax player for *Sopa de Pato*?

My life and fantasies as a quasi-musician in a faraway land were now mostly complete. "Yes," I admitted proudly and happily, "I am the sax player for *Sopa de Pato!*"

———

The eradication of illegal coca production continued to be a major focus of overall US counter narcotic efforts in Bolivia, as it was in Colombia and neighboring Peru. Some areas of Bolivia were permitted to grow a certain amount of coca leaf legally as coca—mostly for chewing by Bolivia's indigenous majority, which was a key part of their tradition and culture and supposed to combat the effects of both hunger and altitude sickness.

Other areas of the country, as in the Chapare, coca production was illegal, though there was certainly plenty being grown every year as evidenced by coca fields being cultivated amidst the Chapare's dense foliage and drying on mats in the sun after being picked.

The reduction of illegal coca, and thus our emphasis on providing legal alternatives for the *campesions* in place of coca, was a worthy goal but at times impractical. No amount of passion fruit, hearts of palm, mangoes and so forth would ever completely replace coca—it grew profusely in the Chapare and there was the cultural aspect to consider.

When describing our efforts to outsiders describing 'alternative development' versus coca, of course we would get the question asking how one could hope to reap returns on legal crops that would compete with the massive returns of illegal coca, even with fancy tropical fruit?

We would repeat the answer of which we first had to convince ourselves. First, we reasoned (somewhat skeptically) that coca growing *campesinos* would prefer to be growing something legal since, from time to time, the Bolivian authorities would burn the illegal coca. And besides, within the long chain of participants in cocaine production, the *campesinos* were not the ones reaping big profits. That was much further up the chain, usually in Colombia.

Finally, there really was good, if not great, potential to develop new, "technified" crops like star fruit, black pepper, passion fruit, and bananas that could be shipped to the large nearby markets of Santa Cruz or, even from there, go by train south to Argentina. The process was aided by sound genetic research into these new and improved varieties, and by improved dissemination to the farmers, either directly or via cooperatives or extension agents. I had seen the same development and then export of high-value tropical and other products in Costa Rica, and the situation was similar in Bolivia.

The annual struggle of USAID and the rest of the Embassy in support of the Bolivian government to limit and reduce legal production of coca was where to get the money to pay farmers to destroy what they were growing. Some of the funds came from local currency accounts, some came from USD accounts that could reimburse the Bolivia government for the use of its own currency, and finally, one year, we used local funds that had accumulated untouched from years of PL-480 food assistance accounts.

By this time in our Bolivia stay, we had a new and experienced Ambassador, and I had moved up to the position of Mission Director, as my friend and mentor who had been the former Director had had to answer the call to fill in the Director's position in El Salvador. So, up I moved though that had certainly not been part of the original plan when we got the Bolivia assignment

I guess I had some initial trepidation at becoming the boss of such a large and politically sensitive USAID operation, but I quickly decided I was too busy to worry about it and plunged into the job. The USAID staff, both local and American, were thoroughly supportive and professional, and so along with the personal challenge, there were a lot of important professional challenges going on too, and a lot of it was fun.

Bolivia was and is a vast country with vastly different zones: the Altiplano above La Paz and merging into Peru; the Beni composed of jungles and Amazonia going towards Brazil; the vast cattle and farming lands of the Sierra in the eastern zone around Santa Cruz; the desert-like Chaco going down toward Paraguay; and wild and rugged mountains and valleys around Tarija going toward Argentina. In between were the valleys around Cochabamba and the far-flung judicial capital of Sucre.

But traveling in Bolivia was not for the faint of heart.

Flying was often a gut-wrenching experience as the plane bounced and rocked upon turbulence between snow-covered Andean peaks. Kissing the ground upon arrival at El Alto or Cochabamba was probably not an acceptable action, but I was always relieved to arrive in one piece.

And the roads were even worse.

Most roads, even between major cities, were scary affairs with exposed ledges dropping thousands of feet. Often you would meet buses headed in the opposite direction, and one of the parties had to figure a way to let the other pass. One foot too far toward the ledge, and it was goodbye forever!

One road, the Corioco road linking La Paz with the town of Corioco down in the jungles many thousands of feet below and down a terrifying narrow strip of dirt road, was aptly called "the most dangerous road in the world." It seemed that there were weekly stories of busses full of passengers plunging into the abyss.

I drove the Corioco road three or four times with a driver—and only when I had no alternative—and I was racked with white-knuckled fear each time. AAA did not exist in Bolivia, and it wouldn't have mattered if it did. White crosses—too many to count—populated the roadsides where unfortunate souls had gone over the edge.

I also drove the family all the way from La Paz to Potosi where the Spanish had worked the world's largest deposit of silver during colonial times. The roads kept getting worse and worse, with cliffs and precipices greeting us with every turn, so I decided to send the family back home to La Paz by plane, while I drove back solo via Sucre, the judicial capital, and Cochabamba.

Between Sucre and Cochabamba my nightmare of driving along a narrow one lane road hanging thousands of feet in the air in the face of oncoming traffic was realized. I came face to face with a bus on a curve which required one of us to back up and somehow make way. With heart beating fast, I backed up a few meters but then motioned to the bus driver that the rest was up to him. He inched backwards near the precipice and I was eventually able to make my way around him to safety.

I resolved to have a pisco sour or three once I had finally made it to Cochabamba and relative safety.

There were a few opportunities for work and family adventure: a group of us flew to Cuzco, the former Inca capital in Peru, and then we made it to the summit of Machu Pichu. It was a world-class, amazing sight.

A group of USAID Mission guys decided to hike part of the Inca trail on a section that started south of La Paz on a mountain top and eventually wound its way thousands of feet lower into the jungle and a road stop where one of our group had pre-stationed his vehicle for our return.

For me, the hike was memorable not only for the spectacular scenery, but because after years of sports wear and tear on my knee, it locked up at a point nowhere near a road or civilization, so I had to fashion a crutch out of a tree limb and slowly advance along the trail. A healthy robust *cholita* happened by and took charge of my backpack while I concentrated on my weakened body. Eventually, we made it to the vehicle, the backpack bearer was rewarded handsomely and, after a thoroughly fine but somewhat perilous adventure, we made it home in one piece.

Meanwhile, back in La Paz, Joy was also working for USAID as a contractor, managing an export promotion project with a Bolivian export association that worked with a variety of Bolivia export-oriented companies. She loved the work and to this day points to her experience in Bolivia as the height of her own professional career.

Though since I was the newly minted boss or Mission Director, such cases as employing the spouse of the Director could fall into the dreaded "conflict of interest" category, she had been hired prior to my promotion and thus reported to someone else. I recused myself from her project and all was copasetic.

All was not wonderful however, as one weekend one of our respected US official managers, a former FBI employee working on a judicial training project, died unexpectedly from a heart attack at the age of thirty-nine. We were all devastated. As a manager, I had to confront the responsibility of leading our response to this tragedy, care for his widow to the extent we could, and comfort the grieving US and local staff.

Personally and professionally, serving in Bolivia was a pretty wonderful departure for the rest of my career as a senior manager for USAID. I was glad to have proved myself as a competent manager and decision maker and my many bosses in Washington seemed pleased, too.

However, after five years and more than two "tours" at post, it was once again time to figure out what to do and where to go next.

It didn't take me long to find out that a Director position was soon to open in far-away Jordan, and that was quickly where I decided I wanted to go. I began the process of letting all the right people in headquarters know of my interest.

This region, after all, was where I had worked so long ago on an archaeological dig, and with a language, culture and history which I had studied, and to which I had been attracted for years. Proximity to biblical sites, Jerusalem and, in the wake of the first Gulf War, the region where, politically and economically, a lot was going on that made me want to participate.

Jordan

I ARRIVED IN THE capital city of Amman late one night several weeks in advance of my family. I had been practicing my very rusty-to-now-non-existent Arabic in preparation for my arrival. My new driver, Sammy, was at the airport to meet me and when I tried to let loose with a phrase or two in Arabic, he looked at me solemnly and said to me in English, "Sir, we don't speak that way here."

I had been told in graduate school long ago that the Arabic they were teaching us (Modern Standard Arabic) was usable and understandable throughout the "Arab World" but that wasn't quite true as it turned out. There were more "classical" Arabic words in my version and that surely wasn't what they spoke in Jordan—or Iraq, or Tunisia, or Egypt or much anywhere else as it happened.

Oh, well, at least I could go through the formal greetings and show enough facility to let folks know I cared enough about the culture and setting to have gone through the trouble—not to mention the work, time and expense—of knowing some of the Arabic basics.

I would soon realize that practically all of my future Jordanian counterparts spoke great English, having gone to school in the US or UK and the country having a background with the British going back to World War I with even a royal tie back to the days of Lawrence of Arabia.

I would continue to study Arabic in Amman one-on-one with a tutor but however more proficient in the language I became, I was never, ever going to be able to converse professionally. I could learn to do better greetings, buy carrots in the open markets, ask driving directions and for the "haman" (bathroom) but the conversation could never go so far as politics or economics.

I liked Jordan from the start and soon came to love much of it.

My first shock, however, regarding Jordan had nothing to do with the language but rather with the USAID program and especially the budget I was inheriting. It was tiny, paltry even, and compared to the ambitious programs we had had in Costa Rica and Bolivia, and it initially took me aback. The USAID official back in Washington who officiated over my swearing ceremony had broken the news during his remarks. I was surprised at what I was hearing.

During my swearing-in ceremony at the State Department—which is a big deal and the USAID equivalent of an Ambassador's swearing in—I decided to test the limits of humor and depart from the time honored tradition of thanking one's parents (mine had passed), the fifth grade teacher, the football coach and so forth.

I said I would like to give special thanks to my buddy in Iraq, Saddam Hussein. After all, if not for his invasion of Kuwait, our evacuation from Tunisia and subsequent successful positing to Bolivia, I would not have ended up exactly where I wanted to be—Jordan. It was tongue in cheek, of course, and my assembled friends at the ceremony took it as intended—with a laugh or two.

I guess I had been so immersed with the details of Bolivia until the very end that I had failed to focus on what was awaiting me in Amman. There was something wrong with this picture. Jordan had signed a real peace treaty with Israel two years back and was now experiencing severe economic problems.

Weeks after I arrived, there were bread riots in the southern Jordanian city of Ma'an and the situation was tense. While the peace treaty with Israel—spurred by King Hussein—was more than positively received by the US, it seemed that rather than providing more material support to Jordan in a time of economic need, it seemed to me that we had just inexplicably moved on.

Jordan then was, and is, one of the keys to what passes for stability in the Middle East. Relations between the US and Jordan had been close ever since the 1950s when a young King Hussein forged a special relationship with the US for mutual benefit; the US gets a key partner in a turbulent region and Jordan gets an ally that could help protect it if and when things went south. Jordan's role as a "buffer state" for Israel could not be denied but we had plenty of reasons to support and defend Jordan notwithstanding Israel. It was "between Iraq and a hard place" we said often, and it was true.

In the run-up to the first Gulf War in 1991, long serving King Hussein—who had known every US President since Eisenhower—felt he had to cater to pro-Iraq, pro-Saddam Hussein domestic sentiment, by speaking far more harshly in Arabic than the more conciliatory remarks he made in English.

Iraq was Jordan's largest trading partner and Jordan provided Iraq with manufactured goods and export outlets. Iraq in turn provided Jordan oil and gas at subsidized prices. Jordan feared the economic impact of losing this source of revenue and especially Iraq's oil.

When the Iraqis occupied Kuwait in its 1990 invasion and were subsequently expelled and defeated by coalition forces in 1991, thousands of Jordanians who lived and worked in Kuwait and formed an essential part of Kuwait's skilled labor force were summarily expelled by the Kuwaitis back to Jordan. The sudden influx of returned Jordanians complicated every aspect of life in Jordan—lack of jobs, housing, and schooling to name a few. Jordan was still adapting to this new reality when we arrived in the country.

For some reason I felt at home in Jordan from the start. As much as I liked a country like Bolivia, at times I would look out at the Andean peaks and realize that I was deep in South America and sometimes wonder, "Where am I and how the heck did I get here?"

Inexplicably, despite all its problems and location in a volatile region, in Amman I almost always felt at home, safe and always fascinated by the surroundings, the history, the biblical and archeological sites and the work. Maybe it was the mind print left over from my archaeological dig in the region as a kid, but maybe it was more...

So much in Jordan attracted me—first, the "land of the Bible" and proximity to Israel and Syria. If not for borders and paperwork, one could drive from Amman to Jerusalem in a bit over thirty minutes.

Those days, at least for now, are over.

Still, it was the land of the ancient Ammonites, of Moab and Edam. There were ruins of ten Greek-era cities in Jordan, called the "cities of the Decapolis", the most compelling being Pella where the apostles supposedly took refuge after the crucifixion of Christ.

There were Crusader castles from the eleventh century, rich Islamic structures and castles from the Ummayyid period, remnants of Christian communities still hanging on from the time when Jordan and the region were Christian. At the time, only about six percent of the Jordanian population was Christian with numbers constantly dropping.

The ruins of the Roman city of Jerash were some of the best preserved outside Italy or North Africa, and spectacular. In Jerash the ruts of Roman chariots and vehicles were clearly visible dug into the stone streets.

I was also constantly intrigued and at peace with the countryside outside Amman—the Jordan valley that represented most of the only ten percent of Jordan that was arable and where the locally produced fruits and vegetables came from. The deserts—most of the country—were empty by one perspective but teeming with intrigue on the other.

I had been presented with a marketing challenge with my spouse about moving to the Middle East, especially with three young children, including two daughters, but it proved not to be a problem. Though there were plenty of Jordanians who were religiously and culturally conservative and would never forget the US's relentless official support for Israel, many, or certainly most with whom we lived and worked, were open, kind and generous and remain so today despite near-by wars and crises.

The Middle East is not always a dark and bloody place, no matter how it is continually depicted by the media.

I soon discovered that I had a kindred spirit with the US Ambassador to Jordan—always a good thing for a USAID Director to find. He was even a Tar Heel with deep North Carolina roots, so we could always talk about college basketball. He and I soon shared our mutual concerns about US assistance levels given Jordan's current economic problems, and we soon discussed what to try to do about it.

We agree that Jordan's immediate problems were lack of economic opportunity (jobs); that there were too many people in a small habitable part of the country; and perhaps most seriously, Jordan was the second water poorest country on earth. "Too many people, not enough jobs and running out of water" soon became our mantra, and what precisely to do about it became our focus.

My Jordanian and US staff I am sure got tired of hearing me talk about it, but it helped that everyone seemed to buy in on the vision and were eager to work together to make things happen.

Needless to say, as in my previous assignments, such strategizing had to be led by the host country Jordanians, not us, and we had to agree on approaches and then work together to figure how to muster scarce resources.

One key event was the visit of a CODEL (Congressional Delegation) led by a New York City Democrat, Nita Lowey, with the able participation of an Alabama Republican who, we were told, had started his professional career as a truck driver. The delegation listened carefully and the Ambassador and I detailed Jordan's serious economic situation in preparation for their talks with Jordanian officials.

My direct counterpart with the Jordanian government was a female Minister (one of the few), smart, US educated and no shrinking violet when it came to expressing her opinion. She was also a Palestinian-Jordanian and this group of citizens—undoubtedly a majority of the population—had previously been systematically prevented from joining the government or military.

This Minister had clearly broken the mold based on brains and determination, but it took some time for her to be convinced that we Americans meant well and wanted to help them with the problems. Or to put it bluntly, as a friend from Kansas used to say, "It's a money problem, and money solves the problem."

The CODEL's meetings with the government, including my counterpart Minister, made a deep impression on the US delegation. The Prime Minister and my counterpart spoke persuasively about the risks they had taken in signing the peace accord with Israel and, to date, the lack of material benefits that had happened to Jordan after the accord. In fact, economic problems persisted—as seen by the Ma'an bread riots—while Jordan's population growth and lack of jobs and water made things worse.

We all admired King Hussein for many of his qualities, but economic reform was not his strong suit. That would come later when his son Abdullah took over, but Jordan was fast reaching the point where a real crisis was emerging. The US, after the perceived too-friendly-to Saddam attitude before and during the Gulf War, had returned to seeing Jordan once again as a staunch ally and a force for what passes for stability in the region, but our economic support for Jordan had not caught up.

The CODEL was impressed by the Jordanians' pitch for more US support. They could have played their hand in any number of ways that could have missed the mark, such as implying that "You owe us" but they stuck to the hard facts, and that turned out to be enough.

Once the CODEL returned to Washington, they started the push to substantially increase our assistance budget—and did so by turning a very modest one into one where our budget increased by some 300% the next fiscal year.

Suddenly—at least "suddenly" in terms of how these things work bureaucratically—we were back in business. This increase was of course in Jordan's best interest but also, given Jordan's regional support and the special relationship we had had with Jordan since the 1950s, also equally important for the foreign policy interests of the United States.

My counterpart Minister of Planning suddenly decided she could put up with me on a more friendly basis—proof that not only did "money talk" but it also changed attitudes—so we earnestly began joint discussions about how best to apply the additional funding.

We soon agreed that an increase in the water sector made infinite sense and decided too to dedicate more funds to creating jobs. Given that Jordan, again, was "the second water poorest country on earth"—I never found out what the poorest one was—and its unemployment rate at over thirty-percent, it was clear that we were choosing the right sector on which to focus.

You can't have a country if you don't have water.

Living with the scarce water situation in Jordan was at first shocking to visitors. The water in Amman was turned on perhaps two times a week and the rest of the time there was nothing. People stored as much water as they could gather in home or apartment cisterns, pumped water to roof tanks, conserved and rationed what they received, and then waited until the water came on again. For Amman's many poor, it was never enough. Richer citizens could order trucks full of water to fill cisterns when supplies ran out, but that was far beyond the financial reach of most of Amman's people.

Our water sector work would include major funding for water treatment, water conveyance, storage, wastewater treatment, repair and construction of water pipelines in Amman and elsewhere, sewage treatment facility rehabilitation and the like. We eventually put many millions of dollars into these water projects and nothing else in my view was more important to Jordan and to its stability.

It would have been hard to keep up with Jordan's growing population's water needs in the best of circumstances, but the problem was made worse by the influx of thousands of refugees over the years: Palestinians in 1948 and 1956—to the point that the majority of Jordan's population became Palestinian—and then more Jordanians expelled from Kuwait after Gulf War I; and then later, after we had departed the country, thousands of Iraqis after 2003 and more waves of thousands fleeing the civil war in Syria after 2012.

Our first water project with our increased funds was a wastewater treatment facility at the southern town of Wadi Musa, the modern town adjacent to the ruins of the ancient "rose red city" of Petra.

Despite my aforementioned praise of some of Jordan's historical and archaeological treasures—and there are thousands of them— Petra is Jordan's most spectacular attraction from the Nabatean period (about first century BC through the fifth century AD) and its premiere tourist destination.

Petra is an immense stone city carved in the rocks with the massive "Treasury" (think *Raiders of the Lost Ark*) and other tombs and temples still standing testament to the rich civilization that existed because it was on the principal trade routes of the time.

As one enters Petra, one slightly descends through the "siq"—a narrow passageway between massive stone walls finally ending at the "Treasury", so-called because post-Nabatean locals believed treasure was contained in a carved stone vessel at the top of the structure. Old bullet holes mark the giant carved jar that has been fired at for years to no avail. As one passes through the siq, there are the remains of clay pipes that conveyed water from "Ain Musa"—Moses' Spring—which was located in the upper part of Wadi Musa and still produces clean, clear water.

The name Musa originated from Moses of the Bible who passed through town during his forty years of wandering with the Israelites. His brother, Aaron, also mentioned in the Old Testament and the Qu'ran, lay entombed in a stone sepulcher high above the siq on a mountaintop, a site revered by Muslims, Christians and Jews alike.

My son and I hiked up to Aaron's tomb in the heat of summer. The two liters of water we hauled with us wasn't nearly enough.

Petra was on the itinerary of every VIP and other visitor to Jordan and soon I was racking up a few dozen visits to Petra, to the point that I could have given—and did conduct—tours of the place, but that story comes later.

It made sense for Jordan to further develop Petra as a world class tourist attraction because, first and foremost, it was like nothing else on earth, and tourism created jobs for the locals and foreign exchange for the economy.

One prerequisite to making the site viable for tourism was to construct Wadi Musa's first wastewater treatment facility, and the fact that our budget had grown substantially made it possible to offer a substantial contribution to the project, which also made me much more popular with my counterpart Jordanian minister who had earlier lamented our initial meager offering.

Traveling to Petra was a dream come true for an amateur Middle East history, religion and archaeology buff like myself. The American Center of Oriental Research (ACOR), based in Amman, also made several major discoveries in Petra during our time there.

The "Petra Church" has beautifully preserved mosaics in the floor, a fifth century nave and alter, and probably best of all, several mostly intact scrolls from the period detailing land transactions, church news and more evidence of daily life in fifth century Petra. Nearby stand four upright columns of Egyptian blue granite that were somehow transported down the Nile, and eventually to Petra.

It took nearly two and half years of work for our contract technicians working hand and hand with our Jordanian counterparts to complete the wastewater treatment plant. When the time for the dedication ceremony arrived, the head of our Agency came from Washington, DC, to represent us.

We made arrangements with the authorities who worked with the Palace to secure a royal helicopter to transport Brian, the Ambassador, myself and the Jordanian Minister of Water and Irrigation—our direct counterpart for the project—to the site. The Jordanian minister's name was Munther, and I took time to explain to Brian before the flight that the Minister was the Christian minister (the Jordan cabinet traditionally had one Christian minister).

I don't know what Brian was thinking but upon landing at Petra his question to the minister startled me. "Mr. Minister, how did your family come to be Christian?"

I think Brian was seeing visions of a Baptist missionary somehow passing through and converting Munther's family sometime a few generations in the past. Of course, this was ridiculous as the roots of Munther's faith were ancient and deep, or as I used to say "Yep, that Jesus fellow, he came from right around here."

Munther pondered the question for a moment and slowly answered, "Well, we pretty much got it directly from our Lord and Savior."

I think Brian quickly realized his faux pas as he looked thoroughly embarrassed.

We liked and respected Brian a lot for many reasons—one was that he saved the Agency from the attacks of a certain US Senator from my original home state—so we decided to give Brian a pass.

It was a hot sunny day and maybe with the heat he just wasn't thinking. In any event, the Ambassador and I agreed that this was one story we would remember.

———————

Working as Director of USAID in Jordan at the time represented one of the highlights of my career.

First, I had a great staff—only eleven excellent Americans but a Jordanian staff of some forty more—engineers, program specialists, drivers and so forth who were smart, dependable and dedicated. Without them we were nothing.

The other two factors were also unique; reforming and quality Jordanian counterparts in both the government and private sector—this was their country, after all, and finally, full support and financing from our colleagues back in Washington. This combination was unique, at least to the degree that it evolved in Jordan, and I was grateful.

I was also learning a few "management lessons" that I thought were valuable: Make the program "a mile deep and not a mile wide"; i.e. choose the top priorities and do them extremely well. Don't try to do everything as you will spread yourself too thin and fall on your own weight.

Do not micromanage staff or programs. Trust and reward staff achievement. Do not expand staff numbers simply because you might be able to afford it. Also, and perhaps most importantly, consolidate and limit management units to assure flexibility and results.

I am sure the staff got sick of me saying "A mile deep, not a mile wide" but they seem to have bought into it.

"Too many people, not enough jobs and running out of water" was the other mantra, and that about summed up what the Jordan program was about.

Soon the budget had grown to the extent that we could undertake more water projects, reinforce health and family planning programs, and dive much deeper into the "not enough jobs" issue, which came to mean supporting the Jordanians own "economic policy reform" efforts, supporting private sector association development, privatization of state enterprises, sustainable microfinance, WTO accession, stock market modernization, regulatory reform (especially easing government regulation governing foreign investment business start-ups), support for export-oriented industries, support for Jordan's nascent IT sector and a hundred other things.

One aspect of living and working in Jordan that I had to learn about was dealing with Royals. I was honored to have met with King Hussein several times before his passing. He was "Your Majesty". Likewise, for "Queen Noor", nee as Lisa Halaby, US-born in the same year as myself.

I also met then Princess Rania ("Your Royal Highness" at the time as opposed to "Your Majesty" as it is now), the spouse of King Hussein's eldest son Prince Abdullah. I even had a couple of meetings with the then Crown Prince Hassan, one with my Washington boss of Petra fame and the other with a World Bank official to discuss our blossoming microfinance programs.

I had sought out Princess Rania (now Queen Rania) as I thought that high-level support for microfinance programs—which, almost by definition, would be concentrated on women borrowers, had to be a good thing. Soon she agreed to help us and added sustainable microfinance along with child education and protection to her list of priorities to support. I remember asking her if we could make her "the rock star of microfinance" and whether I now recall it accurately or not, I think she agreed.

Sustainable microfinance required small loans ranging from as little as fifty dollars to as much as five hundred dollars with interest rates sufficiently low enough for each effort to remain solvent. There was often a "group lending" approach where the group—invariably groups of women—reinforced loan repayment.

Loan funds were used to establish produce stands, sewing shops, chair and tent rentals, jewelry stores, food stands and many more small enterprises.

Prior to this effort, the history of microfinance in the Middle East had been more or less one failure after the other, with loan defaults the rule rather than the exception. These people were just "too poor", went the argument, "to repay," and inevitably each program would collapse as unpaid loans mounted and the financial corpus of funding drained.

So we decided we would only undertake "sustainable" microfinance, and offered training to assure Jordanian managers could execute these programs properly. We first worked with local NGOs that soon established their own separate microfinance units following "best practices". Then we went to work on the formal banking system to convince them to offer small or microloans as part of their portfolios. The lesson was that they could make money doing this and at the same time provide a new service to a whole new client group who under normal circumstances could never get a bank loan.

It was easiest to do microfinance work in the big cities like Amman, but with the assistance of some hardy US NGOs, we helped the Jordanian institution and banks expand to outer lying cities like Aqaba, Wadi Mousa, Tafila, Ma'an and others.

It was a process, but after three years' work, successful microfinance programs had spread throughout Jordan, and we had gone from zero to 50,000 loans, eighty-five percent of borrowers being women, and a repayment rate of over ninety-eight percent.

This was a success of which we were justifiably proud but equal credit went to the scores of hardworking Jordanian NGO members, bankers and many others who were willing to try new methods and lending practices that proved to be sustainable. Microfinance was not the full solution to Jordan's unemployment problem, but it put added income into the pockets of Jordanian families and empowered mostly poor and hardworking women.

Even conservative and traditional Jordanian men became supporters of microfinance in direct proportion to increases they saw in family income. Princess Rania helped lead the charge and provided crucial support for the programs at their beginning.

Working in Jordan on our many activities was quickly becoming the highlight of my career to date. There was a very unique combination at play now: reform-minded and capable Jordanian counterparts; a windfall of financing from Washington; support from our many bosses in DC, including Congress and the State Department; and broad agreement as to the kind of programs we should put in place.

We were also aided institutionally by decentralization of authority to the field which allowed us to adapt and adjust to new realities on the ground without second guessing or micromanagement from headquarters. We reveled in our ability to think a bit "on our feet" in the field. We respected the rules but were also able to work creatively within the system. Besides, I was fortunate to have a great US staff. Final blessing: A capable and compatible Jordanian staff. Without them, nothing much would have gotten done. I think they even enjoyed coming to work most days. I liked the staff so much that I decided to fast along with them during the holy month of Ramadan. It wasn't easy, but I wanted to show empathy and also see if I could do it.

It took me a while, but I finally came to understand that a good portion of the local staff were in fact Greek Orthodox Christians and had no intention of fasting. Joke on me.

———————

I loved being back in the neighborhood of Jerusalem, or "just across the River" (Jordan) as we used to say. Due to extraction of most of the stream's water for irrigation and drinking upstream, the mighty Jordan was not only not a river but barely a creek—and a polluted one at that—by the time it approached the Dead Sea.

The bridge across the Jordan leading up the hill to Jerusalem from Amman was called the Allenby Bridge by the Israelis and the "King Hussein Bridge" by the Jordanians. With my diplomatic credentials it was relatively easy for us to pass through and continue to Jerusalem but not so for the scores Jordanians or Jordanian Palestinians trying to visit family in the West Bank, many finding it impossible to get Israeli clearance to enter, and for others finding the task of crossing to be slow and often tortuous. The Israelis who controlled the crossing and the land took security very seriously. I felt badly for the crowds of Palestinians and their lined-up busses waiting and waiting for a chance to cross and visit family and home.

Going back to Jerusalem brought me back to my seventeen-year-old self, and the places that had first stimulated my interest in an overseas life. I had made a "bucket list" of biblical sites I hadn't seen the first time around, and I looked forward to ticking them off. My first trip back with the family found us staying right outside the walls of the Old City in the Catholic inn Notre Dame.

Run by Palestinian Christians, the hotel staff must have thought that we were more important than we were and assigned us to the Pope's suite, like the "Presidential Suite" but more sacred. We looked at the painted cherubim angels dancing on the vaulted ceiling above us and marveled at our fortune. Smells of spices and freshly washed cobblestone alleys of the Old City brought back vivid memories of the first time I had beheld this amazing place.

The second time we went back to Jerusalem—entire family in tow—we acted as tour guides for Joy's parents who kindly put us all up at the ritzy American Colony hotel with its own history and a nicer place than we would have stayed if we'd been on our own.

The Church of the Holy Sepulcher, the Western Wall, the markets and the hubbub of the city's streets with orthodox Jews passing Christian orthodox priests passing Muslims in traditional robes and kaffiyeh's reminded us of both the holy nature of Jerusalem to the three "divinely inspired" religions and, as well at the same time, to the volatility of the holy city and places, religious torment and hatred on a slow boil just beneath the surface.

As a Christian, the Church of the Holy Sepulcher was my favorite place. Built on the site of an earlier Roman temple to Venus, this was the site of Christ's crucifixion and burial. The site was rediscovered and identified in the year 323 by Saint Helena, the mother of Roman Emperor Constantine, the first Emperor to convert to Christianity. The massive golden dome of the Church above us was being refurbished and we heard that the "edicule" above the actual burial site of Christ was also on the eventual refurbishment list, an event that finally culminated in 2017.

The side rooms and sites most religious pilgrims don't even know about attracted me and I resolved to eventually see them all, even the ones behind locked door and gates and in control of various Christian factions, not always at peace with each other—Greek Orthodox, Syriac, Copts, Roman Catholic, Armenian and so forth—despite the holiness of the site.

One of our Jordan employees back in Amman told me that his family was one of the two Muslim families entrusted with the key to the Church of the Holy Sepulcher—going back to the period when the European Crusaders were expelled from the city. The Muslim families would open the Church's massive wooden door early in the morning and lock it shut in the evening.

Back in Amman, the work we had started with renewed funding from Congress was showing progress. Water sector work—water treatment improvement, water conveyance, wastewater treatment, sewage treatment and much more—continued with great emphasis and much activity by both Jordanian and American experts and with excellent Jordan leadership.

Work with the private sector was also a priority and one where we could have impact especially given dedicated Jordanian leadership and the fact that our checkbook now had a few more pages in it. We helped modernize the local stock market, helped reform economic policies, supported local business associations and helped some of the early Jordanian IT sector leaders get their start.

It was mostly about creating better conditions for generating jobs which Jordan desperately needed to keep pace with its growing population exacerbated by a high birth rate and the influx of refugees over the years from Palestine, the Gulf War and later from Iraq and Syria.

Jordan was indeed "between Iraq and a hard place" and located smack dab in the middle of a very tough neighborhood. The US's commitment to Jordan went back to the 1950s, and despite a few political detours from time to time, at least now we felt that our joint US-Jordanian efforts were bearing fruit.

One area that Washington would not let us touch was work on the Disi pipeline. Disa was located near the Saudi Arabian border not far from Wadi Rum and amounted to a reservoir of ancient fossil water that would be enough to supply Amman for fifty years. This was too environmentally sensitive for our HQ people at the time, though it would have been a godsend for Jordanians.

Our counterparts at the Ministry of Water & Irrigation, to their credit, found a way to do the project anyway with other funds. When I visited the Minister later in 2015 in his Amman office, he told me, "If we hadn't built the Disi pipeline, given the refugees we had to absorb after the Iraq and Syrian wars, this place would have exploded."

In retrospect, given the sensitive environmental nature of the Disi pipeline and the legal and other difficulties it would have caused, it was perfectly alright that another donor or another country helped Jordan build the pipeline, because when the water was desperately needed, the pipeline was in place.

Finally, we decided to support a new generation of private sector leaders in Jordan interested in making Jordan an IT center, thereby providing a new engine for job creation.

———

While all this activity was going on, King Hussein was undergoing treatment at the Mayo Clinic in the US for what was then an undisclosed illness. This was a matter of much concern, rumor and worry in Amman as King Hussein was much loved by most of Jordan's population and the only King that the vast majority of Jordanians had ever known.

After a number of trips to Minnesota for treatment—with King Hussein at the controls of his airplane for the early trips—it became clearer that His Majesty was seriously ill. Non-Hodgins lymphoma was the diagnosis but there was hope that his cancer could be effectively treated and even cured. Hussein returned home to Amman from Minnesota supposedly cured and rode in an open car in freezing rain greeting thousands of his subjects who lined the streets welcoming him home.

Unfortunately, a relapse showed his cancer was back, and after a final trip to the Mayo Clinic, King Hussein came back to Jordan for the last time. He had recently made his eldest son, Abdullah, his successor, the new Crown Prince. This prompted much concern in Jordan as Abdullah was an Army officer and not then well known.

King Hussein passed away on a Sunday afternoon, a work day for us. The nation mourned, black flags flew from rooftops, and funeral music played on the radio. More than a few of our staff were in tears as was much of Jordan.

As sad as we all were by the passing of this special man, we knew that a massive state funeral was coming with most of the world's leaders sure to attend. The Muslim practice of burial very soon after the deceased's passing made it sure that events would unfold quickly, so the entire Embassy began to make plans and scrambled to do our part.

King Hussein had been close to every American president since Eisenhower, and we fully expected to receive three past presidents— Ford, Carter, and Bush 41—plus the current president, Bill Clinton.

One of the hundred things we did was to assign an Embassy officer as escort for each of the former presidents. Given the Texas and past work connections, I assigned myself to accompany Bush 41.

World leaders began arriving at the secure VIP terminal not far from the regular Amman airport. Jordanian government leaders, ministers and other notables were all attired in western business suits but wearing the red Hashemite checked kaffiyah or headscarf.

The sight of a very large and very blue US Air Force One bearing four US presidents landed, and we got our large motorcade into position. I was standing at the foot of the Air Force One stairway with the four presidents standing together on the ramp above me—a sight I will not soon forget.

As they descended I quickly reintroduced myself to 41 and guided him into his waiting black limo as the same thing transpired with the other three. Soon we were off for the twenty-five-minute drive into Amman. As we pulled out of the airport, I noticed various aircraft arriving bearing other world dignitaries.

From one of the recently arrived aircraft, I watched Russian President Boris Yeltsin walk precariously down the stairway of his jet onto the tarmac. That was the last time I got a glimpse of Yeltsin.

King Hussein's funeral took place in a forested palace area on the outskirts of Amman where I'd had my first audience with Queen Noor, where I had first met Princess Rania, and had had other work meetings from time to time.

I told President Bush about our current program in Jordan and tried to answer his questions. I told him about our family back in Austin while he described his own work with Texas A&M University which was then developing the Bush Presidential Library in College Station.

His son, George W. Bush, was then the Governor of Texas and was making overtures about a possible run for the Presidency. As we drove toward the Palace grounds where all the other world dignitaries gathered, 41 told me of his dissatisfaction with a recent news story that had been critical of his son. This was a great man surely, but when it came to criticism of his son, POTUS 41 clearly had thin skin.

The throngs of dignitaries first gathered outside one of the palace buildings as if awaiting further instructions. Prince Abdullah of Saudi Arabia was on the balcony with a gaggle of aides. The Crown Prince of Kuwait with some Kuwaiti soldiers and bodyguards was there too, and their greeting for "my president" was extremely warm, as you would expect after the results of the 1991 liberation of Kuwait from Iraq.

There was a growing crowd of the world's "Who's Who": Tony Blair, Prime Minister of the UK along with Prince Charles, Egyptian President Mubarak, Yassir Arafat, King Juan Carlos of Spain, Crown Prince Mohamed of Morocco, and other European heads of State and royalty. Israeli PM Netanyahu was there mixing openly with Arab and other leaders who normally would not have been thrilled to see him.

France's President, Jacques Chirac, was standing right beside us for a while and I greeted him in my best French. He smiled and was friendly in return, surely asking himself, "Who the hell was that?"

The four US presidents and their aides were loosely hanging out to-gether and starting conversations with their international colleagues and their Jordanian hosts—all males, as the women, including Queen Noor and other female relatives, were seemingly banned to another part of the Palace and definitely not mixing with the male guests.

Dozens of dignitaries and their aides were then directed to enter one of the Palace buildings to await the start of the actual funeral. As the four US presidents made their way down a ramp to the waiting area, who should we pass first but Sudanese President Bashir whose country had just been attacked with cruise missiles by President Clinton, who as current POTUS led our group into the waiting area. No cross words were exchanged but we all noticed the irony as we made our way inside.

It was my job to help and advise 41 as needed and I endeavored to keep him out of any trouble or difficult situations that might befall him, whatever that meant.

President Bush promptly started to work the room, walking up to the world's elites, including the Moroccan Crown Prince, clapping him lightly on the shoulder and saying, "Hi, I'm George Bush," as if anyone there would not have known who he was.

I lost sight of him for a moment as I stopped to greet a friend from the UN and looked up in a panic to see him approach a young man in a brown military uniform and sporting a bushy hairdo standing in the corner.

"Hi, I'm George Bush," he said again, and after receiving a smile in return, made his way back to me.

"What's wrong?" he asked me, seeing my fallen face. "Mr. President, do you know who that was?" "No," he replied, "who was it?" "That, Mr. President, was Muammar Qaddafi's eldest son."

"Well, damn", said 41. "I guess that explains why he didn't pass on his Father's warm regards."

The funeral procession of mourners soon proceeded along a route that culminated in a mosque that held the remains of King Hussein's father and where the actual funeral was to be held—Muslims only. Jordanian soldiers held their rifles at the ready in front of them, wearing the red kiffiyehs. Some had tears streaming down their faces.

In another Palace room after the funeral, I saw Prime Minister Netanyahu actually cross to the other side of the room as Syrian President Hafez al-Assad stood in the middle, the two countries technically still at war. These two did not meet or speak but to see them together in the same room was an indelible image.

President Bush then told me he wanted to make his way across the room to greet Hafez al Assad. On the way, Jimmy Carter, who had had the same idea, jumped in front of us and beat 41 to the punch.

As we waited for Carter to finish his conversation and depart, Bush looked for other people to greet and unfortunately started with Assad's bodyguards who were in the outer circle around the Syrian leader. "Don't talk to them, Mr. President," I whispered. "These are armed thugs; just hang on for a minute."

In the meantime, I couldn't help overhearing Carter's and Assad's conversation—Assad speaking through a translator. "When are you going to come see me?" asked Assad to Carter. Carter, smiling his big grin, replied: "I'll come to see you when you're ready to make peace."

Bush and Assad then got to speak briefly and then, to my relief, 41 moved on. When we finally emerged outside, the aides to the four presidents began to summon vehicles for our departure, and everything seemed to be fine except for one small detail: President Gerald Ford was nowhere to be found.

I found Ford's Embassy aide, my equivalent, and asked, "Jim, where is President Ford?" Jim replied, "I thought he was with you."

"No, I've got *my* president," I replied, pointing to President Bush 41 standing close by.

Apparently, we had lost Gerald Ford.

I made my way quickly down the slope of the roadside into a forested area and away from the crowds above. It was getting late and the increasing shadows showed that it would soon be dark. Ford was nowhere to be found.

My question of the moment: How does one manage to lose a US president?

Finally I spotted President Ford walking all alone down the road within the Palace enclave. Relieved, I asked him if he were alright, and he replied in the affirmative.

"Mr. President, please wait here," I implored as I called the site officer and told him to get a vehicle to our location right away.

Soon a US limousine pulled up and we got Ford inside. I raced back up the hill to reunite with President Bush.

How in the world does one manage to lose a president, I asked myself again?

We proceeded to depart the palace and the funeral, much amazed by the spectacle of what we had just witnessed and by the presence of so many foreign dignitaries that I had perhaps seen on television but had never expected to actually see in person or meet.

All four president plus First Lady Hillary Clinton were taken to the Marriott Hotel, where the five met with and then addressed US Embassy staff and family members. I knew how exhausted they all must be, but each made short remarks and then all proceeded to their limousines to make their way back to the airport.

That was the plan anyway, except President Clinton had to act like President Clinton; i.e. be habitually late no matter what the occasion and no matter who he kept waiting.

Later, after the Asian tsunami in 2006, former President Bush and former President Clinton became friends as together they administered a relief effort, but in 1999, as the entire US entourage was delayed by Clinton's lateness, President Bush 41 was not happy.

I had had a personally and professionally great experience with 41. We spoke of Texas, especially his love for Texas A&M University, my Texas family that had known him for so long and even his World War II Naval pilot training that he had done at my Chapel Hill alma mater back in 1943.

As we reached the VIP section of the airport and arrived at the ramp of Air Force One, 41 proceeded to remove the Presidential cufflinks from the shirt he was wearing and pressed them into my palm.

"Thank you," he said sincerely, and then he was up the stairs and on his way home. True to form, in a couple weeks' time, I received a signed letter of thanks from him, one that I still keep framed in my office today.

The passing of King Hussein was a time of high emotion and drama for the Jordanians, and a source of worry to Jordan's allies. The Jordanian economy still needed support and reforming, and now it was in the hands of King Abdullah, much less experienced and less well known than his father and without his father's political gravitas, to be sure.

With Hussein's passing, it was our role, even more than before, to help assure economic support for Jordan, especially at a time when the stability of the region might be more at risk than usual.

From my perspective, we had some unique positive things going for us: we still had smart and reform-minded Jordanian colleagues in both the government and private sectors; King Abdullah soon showed himself to be very bright and a reformer himself; we had a great and supportive new US Ambassador in Bill Burns, with whom I worked closely on an almost daily basis; we had consistent support from all quarters in Washington—the congress and the administration—especially the State and Defense Departments—and as far as USAID went, we had the structure in place to be able to expand as needed without the need to start programs from the beginning.

To me personally, as had been the case in Costa Rica years before, when all the stars came into alignment, great things could be accomplished.

Before too many months passed, President Clinton traveled back to the region and Jordan. The president was to do his work in Amman with the new King and his government, and then President Clinton and Mrs. Clinton—accompanied by Secretary of State Albright—would look at some of our projects near Amman and then proceed to Petra for further exposure to some of our water sector and private sector programs.

The president was to do his work in Amman with the new King and his government, and then President Clinton and Mrs. Clinton—accompanied by Secretary of State Albright—would look at some of our projects near Amman and then proceed to Petra for further exposure to some of our water sector and private sector programs.

We particularly wanted to highlight our microfinance programs where most of the participants were women. We gathered a large group of these ladies who happily volunteered to show off their businesses—like jewelry repair, furniture rentals, beauty shops, falafel stands and so forth. They were proud and were happy to show outsiders the fruits of their labor. We moved the women to a central area of Amman so Mrs. Clinton and Secretary Albright could visit. It was quite an effort in logistics.

Alas, we hadn't counted on the Clinton's habitual lateness. They were so late for every event that most were cancelled or greatly delayed, and the poor women microfinance recipients were never seen. I felt sorry for our employees who had to inform the microfinance ladies that the VIPs had completely blown them off.

The same pattern repeated at Petra. They spent hours on the phone reportedly repairing things-gone-wrong from prior stops in Israel and the West Bank, and again everything was truncated or cancelled. Since the Jordanian Minister of Antiquities, who would normally be giving the tour to the First Lady was not available, the duty fell to me. Given the time constraints, the Petra tour was cut short too, of course, and her "takeaway" from the tour could not have been very much.

I recall my North Carolina grandmother telling a very young me, "If you can't say something nice about someone, better to say nothing at all."

So, therefore in the spirit of my grandmother, and in the vernacular of Forrest Gump, "That's all I have to say about that."

90

In the midst of a heavy but satisfying work load, and multiple trips to every corner of the country, we knew that we were coming to the end of four wonderful years in Jordan. Still, one more big event was on the horizon that I was not going to miss: the visit of Pope John Paul II to dedicate the newly excavated "Baptismal site of Christ" at "Bethany beyond the Jordan" as it was referred to in the Bible.

The site was newly excavated on the Jordanian side of the Jordan River following ancient maps and pilgrimage accounts from early Byzantine times. The area had been heavily mined during past conflicts with the Israelis just across the "river" (creek was more like it) so demining had to precede any serious excavation. Remains of shrines, churches, monks' quarters and so forth were uncovered as well as steps to the site where John the Baptist had baptized Jesus long ago.

A footnote on John: the Herodian palace where Salome danced and where John subsequently lost his head was not far away, in a place called Macharius in the hills of the eastern shore above the Dead Sea, now also being excavated.

Plans were for the Pope to be helicoptered into the Baptismal site, accompanied by King Abdullah, and by throngs of regional Christians, their numbers decreasing rapidly, who had made the trip from mostly Islamic Jordan, Syria and Lebanon to honor the Pope and witness the event. These enthusiastic crowds were waving flags of the papal colors of yellow and white.

The Pope arrived at the scene and exited it via the now famous Popemobile, in this case driven by a smiling King Abdullah. All our Christian staff were there too, some working the event, others just attending the ceremony. After the blessing of the site by the Pope, the Popemobile drove right past us, literally inches away. Pope John Paul looked elderly but happy and dressed in his white robes and hat.

It was an impressive event punctuated by the last minute interruption by one of our valued local employees thrusting a plastic Dr. Pepper bottle into my hands. John said, "This is holy water that was blessed by the Pope as part of the ceremony. Do you want it?" "Sure," I said and put it aside wondering how a Dr. Pepper bottle came to be at Bethany Beyond the Jordan.

That bottle of Holy Water is part of another story that comes later...

Our family had loved almost every minute in Jordan. Professionally, for me, it was the best, and Joy had had a great job working outside for a local foundation where her boss had been King Hussein's sister, Princess Basma, and all three kids had made good friends and loved their school. Daughter Lindsay had so many Jordanian girlfriends and their mothers who spoke to her in Arabic that she could speak Arabic passably well—better than I even after four years of tutoring. To my astonishment, she could even recite "Goldilocks and the Three Bears" in Arabic.

Our time in Jordan was professionally challenging and ultimately satisfying, and we would have stayed longer if possible, but it was not to be. We needed a place with a high school for Lindsay—leaving for a new school with only one or two years prior to graduation was unfair to the child—and for Joy, after so many years overseas and with aging parents, home beckoned.

We painfully decided that I would accept an offer to be Director in Haiti while Joy went home to Austin with the kids.

I knew the family separation would certainly not be ideal, but such things happened regularly for our military colleagues, and also for those of us in the Foreign Service. To this point career-wise we had been very lucky to be together and in countries with American schools, so we decided to put our heads down and make the best of our soon-to-come, less-than-ideal situation.

Haiti

I HAD LANDED IN Haiti in the late 1970s en route to somewhere else, and had been called there for a few weeks of work from Bolivia in 1994 preparing for the return of the recently deposed President Bertrand Aristide. French speakers in the Latin America Bureau were hard to find so I went there to help.

I was quite well-read on Haiti's history, and Haiti both repelled and attracted me. Interesting culture—more African than Caribbean—spoken French for many Haitians and Creole for the rest, physically close to the US, intractable development issues (but that was our job after all), and interesting history much of which was bloody and violent. Note: when a well-known book about Haitian history was entitled *Written in Blood*, it had to tell you something.

I figured that if I survived, it might be interesting; and from the family perspective, I was willing to "take one for the team" this time around. But I had to admit, the joy and enthusiasm I had had for every other assignment was not there. My family had always been there for me and I for them. Not this time. Having the family with me in Haiti was a non-starter—we needed a decent high school for our daughter and Joy's prior brush with violence in Haiti years before made it clear that this assignment would be solo.

I knew that Haiti was not for the faint of heart. The successful slave revolt against the French that culminated in Haiti's independence in 1804 was unfortunately not the start of peace and prosperity for the Haitian people. Rather, it was the start of continued unrest, revolts and counter-revolts, horrific bloodletting and poverty, exacerbated by almost universally failed governance for the next two hundred plus years, aided and abetted by its equal partner in crime, abject corruption.

I asked some Haitian friends once what the explanation was for Haiti's lamentable track record—Haiti was a "failed state" before the term was even invented—and a few answered, "We were not colonized long enough." In other words, Haiti at independence had not achieved any of the sustainable institutions that kept a country stable and successfully developing and thus was prone to falling back into complete and utter chaos.

But referring to Haiti as a "failed state" was too easy and didn't come close to describing what happened to Haiti and why still today it is a place of wretched and recurring catastrophe, whose history has made it a place whose people are mostly hopelessly poor, where infrastructure is mostly non-existent and failing and where natural disasters strike with regularity.

Formerly the "Pearl of the Antilles" and once one of France's richest overseas possessions, the last two centuries have rendered Haiti so poor that its once rich status was reduced by slavery and revolution to poverty, illiteracy, violence, and the lack of rule of law. On top of that—as if that weren't enough—Haiti was continually hit by hurricanes and other natural disasters finally culminating with a horrific earthquake in 2010 that killed as many as a quarter million people.

I quickly noticed that there seemed to be two types of foreign visitors to Haiti: those who were repelled, frightened and repulsed by the chaos, poverty and violence all around them and made for the exits as quickly as possible (as was the case of my wife given her previous experience there); and secondly, those who more or less came to love the place and the people, "*malgre tout*", despite everything, and tried to see beauty and potential, stayed and tried to make it a little bit better.

Haiti is both blessed and cursed by its proximity to the US. ("So far from God, so close to the US" as another writer once said about Mexico.)

On one hand, trade was easy, US investment could have helped Haiti develop, tourism (which had boomed in the 1960s and 70s) could have bolstered the economy as it did in other Caribbean nations, and the close proximity made it easy for some Americans to single out Haiti as a place where their humanitarian and religiously motivated work could have found fertile ground.

On the other hand, Haiti was periodically violent and ungovernable (not ideal conditions for investment). Ironically, while many foreigners recoil in horror at the excesses of the Papa and Baby Doc regimes of the late 1950s through the 1970s, many Haitians look to those days, at least economically, as the "best of times"—electricity that worked, paved roads, schools and hospitals functioning—not the norm afterwards or even today.

Also, US policy at times has worked against Haitian prosperity and development. (Bill Clinton personally helped to destroy the Haitian agriculture sector by US import price policies in the late 1990s, destroying the rice growing sector and throwing thousands of Haitian farmers out of work.) I heard him admit as much in a Haiti speech after the 2010 earthquake.

Proximity also made for US interference in Haitian affairs—the US Marines invaded and ran Haiti from 1915-1930. The US military intervened again in 1995 to help return the deposed Aristide and again, this time, supposedly for good. Our intervention took a different route, following the devastating Haiti earthquake later in 2010, where many Haitian lives were saved and the country helped to its feet by the US and a host of additional international players.

Not to dismiss the fact that the Haitians themselves were doing their best to decimate the environment, reducing the former "richest island on earth" of the 1700s by cutting down most of Haiti's once prolific forest resources to make charcoal for cooking fuel. Now the hills were denuded of vegetation, rains washed topsoil into the sea and caused mudslides into towns and villages.

One could clearly see from the air the border with the Dominican Republic—green and verdant on the Dominican side, deforested and ravaged on the Haitian side. Haitians were occasionally arrested in the DR for the crime of stealing topsoil to bring back across the border to apply to their own barren plots!

I quickly learned upon my latest arrival in Haiti that we as USAID were not permitted to deal with the Haitian government—not the norm in other places of course—but rather to do all or most of our work via NGOs that dotted the landscape in Haiti. NGOs played the role of partly replacing the function of incapable or non-existent government institutions with whom we would normally have dealt.

"The Republic of NGOs" many called Haiti, because there were so many of them and due to the lack of alternatives as effective work counterparts. NGOs had their place but not as a substitute for Haitian institutions or Haitian leadership, but that imperfect situation was where we found ourselves.

The other reason we didn't deal with the government was because Aristide had been deposed yet again, and the US would not recognize the government put into place after that. Instead, the US had saved Aristide again and flown him into exile in Africa where he eventually settled in Pretoria, South Africa, for some years.

Despite former priest Aristide's election as President, and his adoration by a segment of the population, once in power he proceeded to alienate almost everyone else with accusations of corruption, drug running, and directing hit squads at his political opponents. Or so the stories went.

A particularly effective Haitian form of crowd control during the Aristide era was "necklacing"—placing a burning tire around the neck of the victim.

A crude, horrific welcome to Haiti. And "Other than that, Mrs. Lincoln, how did you like the play?"

Despite everything, I was met upon arrival by the US Chargé (acting Ambassador) and moved into the Director's fine house in the neighborhood of Bourdon, across the road from the leafy estate of the French Ambassador. It was a nice villa, but due to poor security in Port au Prince, and the fact robbery was rampant and everyone—good guys and bad—were armed to the teeth, the situation didn't lend itself to much outside entertainment.

That same "stately villa" would pancake into a hopeless ruin during the 2010 earthquake some years after I had departed it for good, but during my time there, once I was home from work, I mainly stayed there until it was time to go to work again the next day.

My house was near one of the few roads leading to the more upscale part of town, Petionville, and down to central Port au Prince. If I left for the office by 5:30 a.m., all was good and I could cruise quickly to the office. Wait much later and the traffic moved at a slow crawl of the vehicular flotsam, along with crowds of humanity that shared the road going to work or school—half broken trucks, cars with flats, animals on their way to market—just a normal third world chaos that reminded me much more of West Africa than the Caribbean.

I was lucky, too, to have a wonderful driver, Anjou, who was always on time, 100% reliable and seemed to always keep us safe through the episodes of violence, robberies, car-jackings and even kidnappings going on all around us.

Anjou's real name was Jean Claude, the same as "Baby Doc" Duvalier and I just presumed he may have been named at birth after Baby Doc before his exile and had wanted a different moniker as an adult.

More positive glimpses of Haiti were evident, too—the painted public transport buses called "Tap-taps" where images of Jesus shared mural space with Shaquille O'Neal and with many renditions of the US flag.

In my view the most vivid and hopeful image of Haiti was seen in the scores of little Haitian girls and boys dressed in their immaculately clean school uniforms, ribbons and bows in the hair of the little girls, chattering along and happily making their way to school. No matter how trying their circumstances were at home, and how hang-dog much of Haiti appeared, the kids always looked their well-groomed best for school.

God had not completely abandoned Haiti after all.

———————

Our work program consisted of watershed management—to protect Port au Prince's water sources from further erosion and deforestation—food assistance to school kids and others in the population, hurricane recovery from past damages, health and family planning assistance, HIV/AIDS programs, microfinance and much more carried out through our large network of NGO partners.

That mix of a program would normally have been motivation enough for me to travel the country to better understand and support the programs, but I had one major task to accomplish first that was only mentioned to me by my Bureau's management literally as I got on the plane.

"By the way, your predecessor went crazy and hired so many staff that your mission now has the highest staff to program dollar ratio in the Agency," they told me. "So, when you get there you'll need to fire about a third of your staff to get back to something rational."

Such an assignment is no formula for establishing good morale. So I brought in three of my trusted senior staff members with impeccable credentials, including my ace Deputy Alex whom I had known since Mali, and put them in charge of deciding where the cuts should be made. I hated to do this to our staff, many of whom had worked for us for years, and all of whom needed the job. It was painful but we got it done and tried to move on.

Speaking of God, and at times feeling that God may have hop-skipped over Haiti and gone elsewhere, churches and religious conviction abounded in Haiti. Originally wholly Roman Catholic, in the recent decades, a multitude of Haitians had become Protestant, and probably more accurately, evangelical Protestant. Religious feelings ran deep.

One old saying was that "Haiti was 90% Catholic and 100% voodoo." That may have been so, and I could not doubt the strength of traditional beliefs that had come with the slaves from Africa to Haiti.

I decided to not spend one bit of energy trying to understand and witness anything associated with voodoo, though I had the chance, it was not for me. I did not need any distractions.

For better or worse, Haiti was near the US—that 650 miles made one heck of a difference—but it was easy for me to go to DC for work and then tack on a day or two to go home to see the family.

I learned all the airline tricks needed to make this work. I could even take the first flight from Austin early in the morning and get the last flight into Port au Prince that same day. I would be lying to deny missing my family as much as I did, but at least I was close.

One more irony of being in Haiti was that after four plus years of being praised and welcomed on the Hill and the State Department due to the perceived excellence of the Jordan program, representing Haiti was more like wearing a target on your back.

Furthermore, the US Senator from my old home state was still around and this time headed the Senate Foreign Relations Committee. He had not even possessed a US passport until recently and had gone on a tear to have my Agency abolished.

That would have been a big mistake, I always felt, and was glad our boss, Brian—the one of Jordan fame with the Christian Minister—was there to lead the bureaucratic fight to save us.

We eventually prevailed and stayed in existence but Brian paid a price for winning: he had been nominated to be US Ambassador to Brazil and was even taking Portuguese lessons, but the aforementioned Chairman never permitted him to even have a hearing. Nomination: Dead on Arrival.

Haiti used to be a rich place before and during the French colonial period—forested, verdant, a jewel of agriculture—but the simmering evils of slavery promoted a full scale revolt against the French in the late 1700s, finally culminating in Haiti throwing off the bloody yoke of slavery and becoming both the second independent republic in the Western Hemisphere as well as the first free black republic.

As previously noted, Haitian history is full of stories of revolt, revolution and bloodshed. More than ninety-five percent of the forest cover is gone and topsoil washes into the sea after rainfall—satellites can routinely observe this from outer space!

Attempts to reforest Haiti have repeatedly failed, undermined by drought and hunger. Desperate people don't have the luxury of worrying about global warming or preserving the home mango tree when starvation is just around the corner.

One could still see traces of the landscape's former beauty—just barely—but the truth of the matter was that it is a mess, the desperate population having pillaged the environment again and again.

The biggest culprit by far was the practice of making charcoal for cooking fuel. Haiti's reliance on charcoal as cooking fuel is killing Haiti's already feeble economy.

I plunged into the work at the office as I always did but with the realization that it would take more than our modest program to transform Haiti and bring prosperity to the Haitian people.

Therefore, my stories of Haiti were of a different quality and magnitude than other countries and mostly having to do with the exceptional quality of the people I met and worked with, and their aspirations and accomplishments despite formidable obstacles, as opposed to developmental breakthroughs as in other countries. Because of these special Haitians I came to realize that God was alive and well in Haiti, just maybe a little harder to find than other places.

I found that I was one of the people who came to love and appreciate Haiti both because of itself and despite itself. The glass was glaringly half empty in so many ways, but at times it seemed well more than half full too.

Life in Haiti for regular Haitians was hard. Hard to find work, hard to feed and support a family, hard to find decent health care, hard to move around, hard to make ends meet, hard to find and afford decent schooling. Despite that, most Haitians were a resilient lot and many just put their heads down, worked hard and made the best out of their lot in life. Being so close to the US, they only had to glimpse at the television to see the life of plenty that was lived in the US only 650 miles away.

It was no wonder that many risked and lost their lives trying to better their lives by taking to the sea in rickety boats, hoping for miracles and praying the whole way. A few made it, but many died trying; many were caught and returned and some ended up in refugee camps.

Back when immigration to the US was easier, many Haitians of some means made it to the US or Canada, got jobs, worked hard, paid taxes and became citizens of their new countries. They raised their families, counted their blessings and sent money home to their relatives still in Haiti and visited when they could. Estimates were that by the time the earthquake of 2010 hit Haiti, there were some 250,000 Haitian Americans in the US and some 25,000 US citizen Haitians living back in Haiti that had to be dealt with and cared for.

After some months living in Haiti, and despite the horrors and hardships, it was the character of the people that won my heart and won me over. I had joined the legions of Americans who loved Haiti because of the innate goodness of the Haitian people who somehow managed to live and survive and spiritually, if not materially, prosper.

As I used to say, especially after the earthquake, these are some of the planet's most resilient people—but nobody should have to be this resilient.

My appreciation of Haiti began with the staff I worked with every day—all different backgrounds, all colors, all political persuasions, various areas of experience and expertise—and then elsewhere as I began to travel throughout the country to see and understand better the work we were doing.

One of my first trips outside Port au Prince was up the coast to the city of Gonaive, at 400,000 people, Haiti's fourth largest city. The town was on the sea and above it loomed bare hillsides long denuded of vegetation due to charcoal production. When it rained normally, mud washed down the hillsides into the town, but when it rained hard, or God forbid a hurricane passed by, as they did periodically, torrents of mud would barrel into the town burying and destroying everything in its path.

Repairing schools, markets, and other structures was part of our "hurricane recovery" program in Gonaive and other parts of the country, but whatever we and our Haitian counterparts would repair, the next storm or hurricane would tear asunder once again. A few years into the future, Hurricane Hanna would strike Gonaive hard, killing 800 people, burying most of the city again and in the process destroying thousands of homes, pulverizing near-by agriculture and destroying a large percentage of Haiti's productive economy. This would have been a terrible blow for any city, but for poor Haiti and for poor Gonaive, it was a catastrophe.

I kept up my efforts to see Haiti outside Port au Prince—we had ongoing programs in most regions and it was my responsibility to know what was going on. I was happy to fly on a small plane out to the southwest town of Jeremie on the northern coast of Haiti's bottom "claw", where there was actually some tree cover and near to where the five percent of Haiti's remaining forest cover seemed to be located.

One American woman we met there, married to a Haitian, was a local mover and shaker, organizing projects, helping the community, helping a local hospital and even, with her Haitian family, trying to regrow some of Haiti's native forest species from a tree nursery they managed in a protected area outside Jeremie.

Bette Magloire invited us to her villa for dinner that evening, a villa overlooking the sea and boasting a swimming pool and palm trees, and as the sun set, I experienced an idyllic scene that I had never expected to see in Haiti.

Our fellow invitees that evening turned out to be a group of Cuban doctors who were part of Cuba's program to provide medical services to poor locales in Latin American and the Caribbean. It wasn't just the Cuban government being nice people—they kept most of the doctors' stipends for themselves.

I recalled that politics being what they were then, US officials were not supposed to officially meet and interact with the Cubans, but we were all guests at the same dinner, so it was hard to not be at least polite.

There were other non-official Americans there too, plus a few of us from USAID, our Haitian-American hosts and the group of about ten Cuban doctors.

I would have enjoyed the evening but none of the US English speakers spoke French or Spanish, none of the Haitian French speakers spoke much Spanish and the Cubans didn't seem to possess much French or English, so I spent most of my evening in the middle of the group doing my best to translate for everyone. After a few minutes of this, my head was numb and I felt more or less overwhelmed in all three languages.

When I did get to speak privately with one of the Cuban doctors, he told me that in Cuba his monthly salary was about thirty dollars, and for that reason and despite the government taking most of his overseas earnings, it was still an attractive proposition to work outside Cuba. I felt somewhat sorry for the Cubans but they were nice and there was no need to venture into political discussions so we had a pleasant time. As the moon rose over this lovely and tranquil scene, I decided that reality could wait until the next morning.

———————

The next break in our temporary tranquility was the result—or lack thereof—of the US Presidential election between Al Gore and George W. Bush in Florida, and the saga of the "hanging chad".

Many of our Haitian staff had US relatives in Florida and a few were US citizens themselves and registered voters in Florida, so this race was of great personal interest to them.

I had a hard time grasping that counting votes in a few Florida precincts would prove so difficult. To me, having worked on "democracy", "electoral support" and "administration of justice" programs in Latin American for years, this was particularly galling, not to mention embarrassing.

For some reason, the former President of Costa Rica—the quintessential "banana republic" (at least they grew bananas there), Jose Maria Figueres, happened to be in Haiti at the time. I had known him from my days in Costa Rica—he had been Minister of Agriculture then—and we had a meeting in Port au Prince to discuss his ongoing efforts to promote "best practices" on investment promotion worldwide that he had presided over successfully in Costa Rica in the 1990s. I also wanted to catch up on the growing economic success story that was now Costa Rica, and he was gracious enough to agree to meet me.

His assessment to me, said with a big smile on his face when the topic turned to the Florida election recount, "So who's the Banana Republic now?"

Indeed, he was right on target, and to me, after all my overseas working on economic development and improved governance, this situation was sobering, to say the least.

There was no escaping the challenges and dangers of Haiti, as more than a few Haitians were desperately and violently poor, but there was also a cadre of world-class people living and working in Haiti that I came to admire.

One of these was a Haitian-American doctor from Cornell University, Dr. Jean William Pape, born and raised in Haiti, who decided to return home to work when he could have easily stayed in the safety and comfort of the US.

A Professor at Cornell's School of Medicine, Bill Pape is now in his fourth decade on the front lines of every major health issue to hit Haiti since the 1970s. In the time that Dr. Pape has been on the job, Haiti's child mortality rate was cut in half, the HIV rate decreased from 6.1% in 1993 to less than 2% today, and overall life expectancy has risen by about ten years. Much of that success is thanks to Dr. Jean William Pape.

When he was a young internist at Haiti's State University Hospital, he was confronted with an epidemic of infantile diarrhea. The mortality rate was a staggering forty-four percent. To combat it, Dr. Pape developed an oral rehydration mixture, which he taught mothers to prepare at home. It worked so well that the mortality rate fell to less than one percent. Within one hour, the child who had been dying had come back to life. It worked so well that Dr. Pape turned his attention to adult patients who presented with diarrhea. These turned out to be Haiti's first HIV/AIDS cases, though the term "AIDS" had yet to be invented.

To battle Haiti's first HIV/AIDS cases, Pape teamed up with colleagues back at Cornell to create GHESKIO, which is now the second oldest research institution in the world dedicated to the fight against HIV/AIDS and which my agency had decided to support some years before. (HIV/AIDS had become so prevalent in Haiti that a myth arose that being Haitian was a risk factor for the disease!)

But Pape and his team produced groundbreaking studies that helped disprove the widespread notion that Haitians were especially susceptible to AIDS. Further, at his insistence, Haiti's Ministry of Health closed all commercial blood banks after Pape's team connected blood transfusions in Haiti to infections. Dr. Pape called this the most important measure taken early on to control the AIDS epidemic.

Soon after my first meeting with Dr. Pape, his GHESKIO center began providing life-saving antiretroviral medicine to Haitians for free and soon after that Haiti was able to turn the corner in the fight against HIV/AIDS.

Haiti was always a study in stark contrasts—violence, corruption, failed institutions, poor medical facilities, and discontent from Haitians who knew what they were missing. On the other hand, schools functioned, people got married and were serious about religion, periods of relative economic and social stability broke out, and just when hope seemed to have vanished, hope (or something like it) appeared again. What a place!

I could have stayed longer than I did, but the kids were at crucial points of college or high school then and, as had been the case too often in the past, I was not around. The Foreign Service, like the military, could not always offer the opportunity for families to be together, but for me, this time, I needed to move on.

Little did I know at the time, however, I was not nearly done with Haiti and Haiti, it proved later, was not nearly done with me.

Kuwait and Iraq

I CONTINUED TO WORK internationally, although based partly at home in Texas and partly in Washington, DC, with periodic travel to both Uganda and Jamaica.

I was actually home in Austin one lovely September morning doing work with an occasional glance at the news online. A headline emerged stating that a small plane had flown into the World Trade Center. That headline was soon to be more accurately updated.

As I wondered what that could possibly be about, Joy called me with a simple message: Turn on the TV.

I sat there transfixed, like millions of others in the US and beyond, as an airliner—the second one—plowed into the other World Trade Tower, both towers soon to collapse into a hellish inferno.

The world had changed forever.

Just the week before, we'd sat with friends on my deck at home and reflected on our amazing good fortune. The country was at peace, the economy was alright, we were free, our children were safe, the water came out of the taps on demand, the power never went out and the garbage man always came on Thursday. We acknowledged that times were good and we were some of the most fortunate people on earth.

After over two decades living and working overseas, and given the craziness, poverty and challenges of the developing world, I felt more than qualified to confirm our good fortune living in our country and the State of Texas. It was certainly true that nothing could make us appreciate what we had like living overseas for over two decades. Or as I found myself saying to our kids every so often, "If you're born comfortable and in the US, you have already won the lottery of life. Don't forget it and act accordingly."

And then 9/11 happened and tore our world and the world of countless others asunder.

I kept working, and kept my eyes on the unfolding aftermath. The

US made its first military responses in Afghanistan with more to follow. After several months passed, we started reading and hearing more about possible US actions against Iraq. My buddy Saddam wasn't cooperating with UN weapons inspectors again, there was talk about "weapons of mass destruction" and tensions were slowly and constantly rising.

A few of my senior Agency colleagues in DC began to talk to me about Iraq. What would the Agency do if in fact there was a conflict there? We knew USAID would have an important role if the conflict happened—most probably on repair of essential infrastructure and other work to get post-conflict Iraq on its feet—but for the present we could do nothing but speculate.

The head of USAID and I started to meet at his DC office. I had a good reputation, as well as Middle East experience stemming from Jordan, but Andrew and I had never met personally. Our mutual colleagues arranged a meeting with him.

Andrew was an international development expert in many fields and in a prior incarnation during the Bush 41 years had been the head of our Office of Foreign Disaster Assistance, USAID's humanitarian and food relief branch. His development knowledge beat anything I had seen from any prior Administrator, and to me he seemed the perfect man for the job he now had.

There were a couple of less-than-ideal factors for him and the Agency at the time though. Compared to the heavyweight Department of Defense, led by Donald Rumsfeld, and the Department of State, led by Colin Powell, we were comparatively small potatoes.

One of the reasons I had avoided serving in Washington to this point in my career was that I loved working in the field, because that was where the development rubber actually met the road; and I hated the thought of being part of the bureaucratic turf battles that characterized working in Washington.

Andrew and I began to speak often, and it was clearly a part of the plan for me to be considered as USAID's point man in the field for whatever was to happen post-conflict in Iraq. We actually had no idea if there would even be a conflict, but it was absolutely incumbent on us to start to prepare for what we would do if there in fact was one.

Andrew understood clearly that we were staring a huge undertaking in the face. Look at World War II, he told me. The US had had years to plan the post-war occupation of Germany and Japan. In Iraq, if a war happened, then we would have far less time to put a program together. Andrew recommended that I read two books about how the US planned and organized our efforts in post-war Germany and Japan, so I knew this matter was weighing heavily on his mind.

This chapter is not meant to be a definitive story of post-conflict Iraq reconstruction. There are plenty of books out there that tackle that subject. I had "no visibility" on the entire gamut of activities anyway, though I came to play a key role in the effort. I write about my experience, and that of my staff, only.

As time went on, it seemed that my Washington bosses were looking increasingly at me as the point for what the Agency would be planning and executing in the field. I was soon to understand that our Agency was not driving this train at all, at least not as a main player. That role was for DOD and State, and increasingly it seemed to me that Secretary Rumsfeld was the one in charge, for better or for worse.

My name was somehow submitted into a very non-transparent bureaucratic maze and eventually, I was told, that Rumsfeld agreed that in the case of an Iraq conflict aftermath, I was to be in charge of the "reconstruction" portfolio.

I was further told by someone who seemed to know what he was talking about that I was in fact not the first choice for the job; not even the second, third or fourth choice—but the eighth!

I somehow emerged as number one, I presumed, because I had been a senior USAID manager in the Middle East previously, had by this point some twenty-four years overseas management experience, spoke some Arabic and additionally was somehow deemed "politically correct".

It also made perfect sense that the US's agency that normally handled this kind of work abroad should be represented and involved at a high level but, that said, the process was anything but clear.

A small cell of people was formed that began planning what a post-conflict program would look like. We were behind the eight ball from the get-go as getting complex programs online in the field required adherence to our procurement guidelines—projects and grants had to be designed and then competed, evaluated and then finally awarded—a process that could take many months.

And if the conflict happened, "many months" is exactly what we did not have. In addition, we would have to identify scores of internal personnel to manage these contacts and grants, and all these people would require security clearances not already in the system and not already cleared.

If that were not enough, how could we competently plan to implement projects in Iraq when we had so little knowledge and information about the country—the infrastructure in all sectors like roads,
ports, bridges, oil refineries, factories, power plants, water, sewerage
and the like? We couldn't even tell how many miles of paved roads
there were in the country at this point, and Saddam and his cronies
were not likely to tell us.

We were mostly deaf, dumb and blind going in, and it was clear
that our approach had to be to identify major, wide-open sector
programs—like infrastructure, health, education, local governance,
economic governance reform and the like, and that had maximum
flexibility permitted within to adapt to, as we began to say often,
"realities on the ground" once we were on the ground.

Clearly this was going to be an imperfect process and by necessity
put together as rapidly as an imperfect system with often inflexible
procurement rules and requirements would permit us.

Hiring personnel to run these programs in the field was another
challenge. Our regular personnel system was wholly inadequate to
provide us the people we needed with the right experience and skills,
so we had to go another route. A special hiring contract was put into
place that permitted us to hire people totally outside the regular
personnel process. It was quick, sometimes dirty, but we slowly began
to assemble a team of professionals who could, we hoped, manage
this beast in the field if we even made it that far.

We were truly flying by the seat of our pants as our "regular"
personnel and procurement systems could not have come close to
meeting our immediate needs.

I should say something about the "weapons of mass destruction"
issue that, as I write this account, has been thoroughly discredited
and therefore seemingly undermined the entire rationale for what
became the Iraq conflict.

The truth was that every intelligence agency out there had concluded that Saddam had these weapons, and based on the gassing and
genocide of the Kurds and Shia in Iraq after Gulf War I, we assumed
that Saddam would not hesitate to use them again.

The point that is sometimes not appreciated by current day Iraq
second guessers, is that Saddam acted as if he possessed WMD and
that added to the allies' determination to confront the problem.
After Saddam was finally captured in late 2003 and began a series
of interviews with his captors, he confirmed why he had acted as he

did. He needed his immediate regional neighbors, especially Iran, to think he had the WMD. To act otherwise would have demonstrated weakness and vulnerability—and Saddam had made a career of being a regional bully: witness the horrible Iraq-Iran war of the late 1980s when millions were killed on both sides, with no good advantage ultimately gained by either side.

Personally, I was in no position to second-guess the WMD assessments and we were all too busy to doubt anything or do much about it anyway. We were expected, at the end of the day, to do our duty, salute the flag and go forth. If we had fundamental disagreements with policy, one could always resign and walk away.

At this point I had worked for both Democrat and Republican administrations and there were inevitably things I didn't personally agree with policy-wise from both groups. But the disagreements were never enough to make me quit my job. So, in this, the case for Iraq, we didn't ponder it too much or for too long. It was our job to get ready despite being far behind in pulling something like this huge task together at all, and much less do it professionally and competently. We saluted and got back to work.

My role as head of "reconstruction" in Iraq was to be, as part of a new DOD-run and established organization called ORHA, the "Office of Reconstruction and Humanitarian Assistance". I was the "Deputy for Reconstruction". There was another "Deputy for Humanitarian Assistance", and a third one for Governance.

The newly appointed head of ORHA was to be a retired US Army Lt. General named Jay Garner. At the time, USAID tended to keep its distance from the military and vice versa, but both groups eventually determined that each organization had different but complementary skills and that since we were all in the same "theatre of operations", we were better off working together than working separately.

Before long, the mantra of "defense, development and diplomacy" being the legs of a three-legged stool, we should understand how essential to ultimate success it was to work together, though at least at the start of the Iraq conflict that was far easier said than done.

Some of my USAID colleagues recoiled at the thought of close cooperation with the military, and many in the military with whom we would be expected to work, had never even heard of us.

General Garner was recently retired from the US Army but had had a sterling track record. As the head of "Operation Provide Comfort" in the Kurdish region of Iraq after Gulf War I, Jay had led an international relief program that saved the lives of thousands of Kurds. To the Kurds, Jay Garner was a hero of the first order, and his contributions to the Kurds' survival would not soon be forgotten.

I first met Jay in the Gulf country of Qatar. I had convinced my Agency bosses to let me go alone to the region, in advance of those to come later, to assess the situation from Kuwait—where our operation would initially be based—and start to plan how we would operate our initial program from there and meet many of the people and organizations with whom we would be cooperating—the Kuwaitis, US military officials, UN agencies and so forth

I arrived at the airport in Kuwait and was met by two US Army majors, one of whom I had known in Jordan. He told me bluntly that I was the first US civilian official to arrive "in theatre".

Soon the word came from Washington that General Garner was to make his first foray to the region, starting at the forward Centcom (Central Command) headquarters in Doha, Qatar. I was told to get on a plane, meet Garner in Doha and take it from there.

We met in the lobby of one of Doha's ultra-modern hotels and proceeded on to the US base at As Sayliyah as it was then called to meet with Centcom commander Gen. John Abizaid.

The two generals knew each other. General Abizaid, who years later would be named US Ambassador to Saudi Arabia, was a descendant of Lebanese Christians, spoke decent Arabic and had a deep knowledge of the Middle East.

Our meetings went well and best of all to me, Jay was open and accepting of a non-military colleague like myself. I had the distinct feeling that this was someone with whom I could work.

Jay and I returned soon after to DC, I to help work on plans for "post-conflict reconstruction" and Jay to stand up ORHA based in the Pentagon. My days in DC were spent making staffing decisions, helping to conceive the content of the reconstruction activities, and helping get work plans in good shape.

It was clear from the start that the centerpiece project for us would be one for basic infrastructure repair in Iraq. We were half-informed that Saddam had let much of Iraq's infrastructure—like power, water, port facilities and so forth—fall into disrepair. We knew too that war planning was to minimize further damage to the infrastructure situation if it could be avoided, and if the potential targets were not key to a positive military outcome. We figured that the key infrastructure that we would focus on and were vital to restoring Iraq's functional economy and to avoiding a post conflict humanitarian crisis, would not be to repair war damage; rather, it would mostly be infrastructure that had degraded as a result of utter neglect from the Saddam regime.

As soon as possible we bid, competed and awarded the infrastructure contract, and the winner was Bechtel. There had been a rumor that we had somehow picked Bechtel for the award from the start and that the contract was not even competitive, but that was not the truth. The contract was the largest that USAID had ever awarded to that point, and it was fully competitive following our procurement regulations.

An independent USAID review board judged all the submitted proposals, and I was appropriately not part of the process.

I was told later that one of the strengths of Bechtel's proposal was that they planned for a major portion of the work to be performed in the field by local Iraqi contractors—a key element in supporting the local economy and getting skilled Iraqis back to work rebuilding their country.

ORHA went about getting organized themselves out of the Pentagon and putting together seminars and training programs. I was surprised—maybe I shouldn't have been—but the process of finding work space in the Pentagon was chaotic, time consuming and killed much of the planning that the non-USAID part of ORHA should have been doing.

I talked to General Garner and my many USAID bosses and convinced them that my place was back in Kuwait where I had already been and where I had a pretty good idea of what needed to be done to set us up there, meaning at least the USAID portion.

I departed once again for Kuwait, got settled into a hotel and got to work. In mid-January I watched a big USAIR Boeing 757 land in Kuwait City with ORHA personnel aboard.

Ready or not, we were there, still not certain if or when a conflict would start, but from the looks of all the material flowing into Kuwait, it certainly looked like a question of when rather than if.

All in ORHA were briefed, issued chem-bio suits and gas masks and soon inoculated against anthrax in case Saddam dropped some WMD gas. We were certainly preparing for the WMDs, though years later the media would treat it all as a sham, and as if we had known that there were no WMDs all along. We didn't.

The evening after receiving my anti-anthrax shot, I went to the nearby US DCM's residence (Deputy Ambassador) for a reception for some of our top diplomatic and military colleagues, many of them non-US. Adult beverages were actually served, which was permitted for diplomatic functions; otherwise Kuwait, like Saudi Arabia, was a completely dry country.

I left the reception a bit early as we started receiving reports of an incoming major sandstorm, and also I was not feeling well. I started my car and headed the quarter mile back to the hotel when the sandstorm hit, and just as I started to feel very poorly.

I inched my way slowly forward in the sandstorm darkness. I thought I had made it nearly back to the hotel, and I abandoned the car where I hoped would be close enough to find the hotel entrance and not block any other vehicles. I made it to my room as quickly as I could manage.

In the room, I must have passed out as all I recall is going from waves of fever followed by intense chills. When I was conscious enough to survey my room, I had moved all my clothes onto the bed for warmth, and then thrown them to the floor when the fever hit again. I had never felt this bad.

I wasn't conscious enough to call the hotel desk or ORHA and ended up being in this state for over two days. When I finally was able to open my door and peer into the hallway, there was a "do not disturb" sign on my door that apparently the male hotel service fellow (no female maids allowed) had placed after seeing me comatose in my room.

Why he didn't alert anyone to my condition, I could only guess.

After two days of this, I was finally able to call Jay Garner, who immediately sent a physician to help. I was still dazed but according to the doctor, I was one of ten thousand who had had a bad reaction to the anthrax vaccine

"The conflict", as we referred to it, started in mid-March, and for us in Kuwait, we were beset with air-raid sirens going full blast and telling us that Iraqi missiles were heading our way. One air raid siren went off as I was driving back to ORHA's headquarters. My cell phone was ringing too. "Get your chem-bio suit and gas mask on" was the message.

This presented me with a quandary. To obey I would have to move off the highway where drivers were driving at breakneck speeds on the best of days and put myself in danger, pull the suit out of the trunk and then spend precious time pulling on my yellow chem-bio outfit and mask and then driving with a gas mask on the rest of the way to ORHA.

I decided I was not going to drive 100 mph down the Kuwait highway with a gas mask on; rather, it was pedal to the metal until I made it to ORHA's HQ and into what was supposed to be a secure area. Once the all-clear sounded, we could get back to work, but we were supposed to leave the gear on. I had a photo for a while of the staff and me writing our daily reports to Washington in full chem-bio gear, masks and all!

The sirens continued to wail, and the Iraqis were in fact sending missiles our way both day and night. Those in charge of our hotel were doing their best to be prepared for a gas attack—the outside of the place was completely bubble-wrapped, making it as gas proof as possible.

The worst incident happened at about 3:00 a.m. when we were back at the hotel and supposed to be sleeping. The sirens went off and a tremendous whoosh swept over us. The hotel shook, and a distant explosion was heard.

The next morning we found that the Iraqis had fired a Chinese Silkworm missile at us which had crashed into a pier a few miles downrange. To be so attacked at night when you were most vulnerable was a scary event for all, but we were relieved that no one was hurt and only the faraway pier appeared to be damaged.

We heard officially that the Iraqi port of Umm Qasr was now in coalition hands, most of the fighting carried out by the Brits. We knew that we would be repairing any serious damage to the port as this was the best way to import large amounts of food and other aid to Iraq to head off a post-conflict humanitarian crisis.

As soon as the coalition authorities judged it safe enough to travel to Umm Qasr for a recon trip, we were off in a multi-vehicle convoy. There was damage to the port cranes and other essential equipment but it appeared that "war damage" was not extensive. On the contrary, most of the damage again appeared to be from utter neglect. Such findings became commonplace across Iraq.

Our convoy pushed through a very dusty and hangdog city of Umm Qasr, stopping to view and photograph one of many Saddam billboards that seemed to be everywhere—in some he was in Western dress brandishing a shotgun, in others he wore full Arab robed regalia.

We noticed that all the billboards had been defaced by the locals once the fighting ebbed: the Shia south hated Saddam due to decades of persecution from the regime including the deadly killing inflicted by Saddam on the Shia after their short-lived rebellion following Gulf War I in 1991. Similarly, all the Baath Party offices we saw were also looted and destroyed. I found a certificate in the ruins praising Palestinian "martyrs" who had attacked Israel, which I rolled up and kept as a souvenir.

The streets on Umm Qasr were largely deserted except for gangs of little boys who ran after us everywhere asking for treats. We recrossed the border and drove back to Kuwait City to wait for more developments. We had made our first entry into Iraq.

We followed events unfolding in Iraq as best we could. Coalition troops made good progress and we listened to accounts of bombing in and around Baghdad. We knew our future ORHA headquarters had been identified—one of Saddam's many palaces—and we hoped it would be spared bomb damage. We knew it was going to be complicated enough as it was once we moved to Baghdad.

I did move on April 23, flying with two other ORHA officials on C-130s from the Oklahoma National Guard. Texans and Oklahomans always bantered at each other, but it was mostly out of good natured mutual respect, though many would admit that respect was diminished a bit on Texas-OU football dates. I told the pilots where I was from and they quickly reminded me UT had lost the past few games to the Sooners, but no matter.

We arrived at a nearly deserted and quiet "Saddam International Airport" (why did he name everything after himself?) though we knew that the airport had witnessed heavy fighting a couple of weeks before as US troops were making their final push into Baghdad. It was in our plans to repair the airport and make it functional again, but judging from the damage to the terminal and tower that I saw, I knew that would require a major effort.

The vehicle picking us up was manned (or more accurately womened) by an ORHA staffer or two, both nervous, wearing helmets and both packing pistols. I guess I'd never before been in a war zone, though Haiti had seemed to qualify as one on many occasions.

The immediate objective was to make it to the soon-to-be famous Green Zone and then move to our new quarters and offices at "The Palace", as it came to be known.

Some palace! The place was a wreck. Most of the furniture was missing, offices were in chaos, no electricity or water and the entire place was covered in reddish dirt and dust.

There was a big mural of Saddam at the entrance that had been covered up by our guys, but there was no covering up the huge metal busts of Saddam that adorned the roof corners of the Palace outside. Other parts of the Palace were just weird—paintings on the walls of Iraqi-flagged Scud missiles being launched, a few pieces of gaudy furniture and overall a style, or lack thereof, that could only be called garish.

So, we had arrived—most ORHA folks were still in Kuwait—but we basically had nothing. We had no water, no food, and no place to sleep, and being late April it was hotter than what I imagined hell to be like. Welcome to our new home, "The Palace"!

While we pondered our fate, a truck arrived carrying a load of bottled water followed by another one with mattresses, followed by another with boxes of MREs, the modern US military's version of C-Rations.

"MREs" stood of course for "Meals Ready to Eat" but many of us thought a better translation was "Meals Rejected by Ethiopians", and no offense intended at all to Ethiopians.

MREs came in various flavors, some of them edible and some disgusting. They were absolutely packed with calories to benefit young soldiers humping in the heat, and not so much for the likes of us in ORHA, but that was what we had. How long would it be before we had a culinary alternative?

While the numbers of ORHA people in Baghdad grew slowly, our challenges did too. The US military was obviously carrying most of the weight for the immediate post-combat phase.

What was being done, I asked, about clear communication with the Iraqi people? Was this ORHA's job, or were we military coalition partners? I knew how vital it was to be in touch with Iraqis to communicate on a thousand issues, and I hoped someone was doing it, because as far as I knew, it wasn't ORHA.

Internal communication, too, was almost impossible. Cells phones did not work, there was certainly no internet (having electricity would have been a nice start) and certainly no computers or connectivity, at least not in the early days. I was given a satellite phone but it only worked outside and incoming calls were hard to arrange in advance so that one knew to be waiting outside.

I did manage to call our Washington office by sat phone once we arrived, and my call was greeted with much shock, shouting and attention on the other end. It was impossible to hear much on my end because a US Army helicopter was flying directly overhead firing salvo after salvo. I imagined this dramatic background effect elicited some stark reality back to our DC colleagues, but it made for lousy communications.

I wondered just how much we could get done in "reconstruction" given the realities that we were dealing with on the ground. One morning was spent running from office to office in the Palace claiming them for our use by placing yellow stick-um notes on the door. Sometimes these would remain in place and sometimes they were replaced.

Our living situation slowly improved but my main memory from that time was a conversation I had one-on-one with General Garner. He said, "This is not our country, we are not here to occupy it for long or try to run the place. This is Iraq, and it must be run by Iraqis and turned back over to them as quickly as possible."

"What about the Iraqi Army?" I asked, a two-million-man strong force at one point and one of the largest such forces on the planet. Jay said very clearly, "We need to assure that these guys continue to be paid and under a certain level of ranking officer, turn these people into allies. They can be used to rebuild the country—their country—and then as soon as possible, we can go home."

Jay and I agreed on that wholeheartedly. A long term coalition occupation of Iraq was wrong and was bound to go bad. We wanted to put an Iraqi face on the whole affair as quickly as feasible and then let the Iraqis put Iraqi substance to accompany the Iraqi faces. We knew we should protect their stability, help reconstitute essential infrastructure, especially power, water and oil production, help Iraqis establish better economic governance and institutions and then go home. I knew it wasn't going to be easy, but the last thing that was needed was a long-term US occupation of Iraq.

Soon I grew weary of my lack of ability to effectively communicate with our people in Kuwait and DC, so I caught another C-130 back to Kuwait where we continued the inflow of our own internal, security, project and contractor personnel to stage and prepare for their entry into Iraq.

We would accomplish this in stages, people going in by both C-130 and vehicle. Thank God one of our DC-based planners had the good sense to order us a small fleet of fully armored vehicles. These would prove to be literally lifesavers in the conditions we would find in Iraq. Most of the rest of ORHAs vehicles sitting in Kuwait were thin skinned (unarmored), tan-colored US SUVs that were fine on good roads but, as fully unarmored, very deficient for many of the tasks ahead.

As work proceeded back in Kuwait, we began to be besieged by US press wanting to know the inside scoop of what was going on in Baghdad. It was part of our job to communicate with the press and get our story out—but we had no control over their true intentions or the stories they ultimately wrote. Many journalists, we were soon to find out, were not really interested in what we were doing, choosing instead to put their own spin on our news.

We now had a core of "public diplomacy" staff both in DC and the field writing detailed daily reports of what we were up to, results achieved and programs underway, such as repairing the power sector, water infrastructure, repairing schools, kids' vaccinations and a thousand other things that were getting underway. The problem was that much of our reporting was not making the news back home. We knew that this was true as our families and friends back home who received our daily reports directly were not seeing anything at all similar in the regular news and wondered why not.

As we added more and more people and organizations to our distribution lists, that helped a bit to get more of the story out, but still the lack of reporting of our work, particularly of our repair efforts to essential infrastructure, just wasn't being reported. It was clear enough as well that some journalists had their own agenda, such as the reporter from the *LA Times* who literally was trying to put words in my mouth in an obvious attempt to criticize General Garner.

It was during this brief stint in Kuwait that we started to hear rumors that General Garner was possibly on his way out to be replaced by another DOD Secretary Rumsfeld choice who, we joked, "looked good in a suit".

I hoped it wasn't true, as I liked and respected Jay. We worked well together and he was always supportive of our mission as part of ORHA. I also knew that Jay, as mentioned already, wanted to make our stay in Iraq as short as possible and get the Iraqis back in charge.

I wondered if the new guy would feel and act the same way.

When it came time to return to Baghdad, this time I joined a US military led convoy and drove all the way from Kuwait City to Baghdad in my FAV (fully armored vehicle). The considerable weight of the armor made it necessary for me to refuel from jerry cans often, which exposed us to enemy combatants who were definitely out there and had already ambushed some of our coalition colleagues, including a valued Japanese friend.

We arrived back at the Palace in Baghdad exhausted but in one piece and quickly assessed what had happened in our absence. The Palace was a much changed place, some communication capability now in place, many military colleagues operating computers in the offices and common rooms, the start of a cell phone network being put into place, a cafeteria, a couple of shower trailers, some trailers in the back lot set up for sleeping where some our staff was now lodged, and best of all, several huge generators that were pumping power to run everything, even a few air conditioners. Iraqi civilians had been hired as workers and many were clearing debris away from the Green Zone.

Most important for our reconstruction duties, contractors for several of our largest projects were arriving and setting up shop throughout the newly named "Green Zone", probably the most prominent space being occupied by the people from Bechtel who were arriving in force.

I had surveyed the Bechtel compound space during my first trip to Baghdad as it abutted the palace-like home of one of Saddam's notorious sons, Qusay, who had fled in the wake of the invasion and was, as of then, yet to be found. Soldiers who liberated Qusay's compound told of finding cases of fine liquors, crates of Cuban cigars, mounds of cash in US dollars and a large cache of pornography.

One of the first things Bechtel did was to engage scores of Iraq subcontractors who knew the terrain and were very eager for the work, be it repairing water conveyance systems, fixing schools—some of which had been used as weapons storage by Saddam—surveying damaged telecommunication infrastructure and the like. One Iraqi sub-contractor told us, "We never got work like this under Saddam."

My opinion of the Bechtel group was always positive—they were highly professional and capably led—and later when the insurgency started in earnest, I used to watch the Bechtel personnel get in their non-armored vehicles, don their helmets and flak jackets and leave the protected Green Zone to carry out their reconstruction work, undaunted and uncomplaining.

In fact, for the first months following "liberation" and our entrance into Baghdad, the city was calm, and very early on, almost devoid of traffic. We would fearlessly ride around Baghdad running errands and even having dinner a few nights at the old Sheraton Hotel in the center of town.

We had arrived after the spate of looting, especially at various Iraqi Ministries, that first erupted after the "liberation" when coalition troops failed to intervene, and of course no Iraqi police or troops were around to enforce any sort of authority. We visited one Ministry—Education, I think—and everything remotely useful had been looted. This meant all files, furniture, fans, appliances, office equipment —everything—had been looted. To my amazement, even the light fixtures and electrical wiring had been stripped from the Ministry walls. This looting scene had been repeated across town, complicating Baghdad's recovery.

Most of the damage to Baghdad had not been a result of fighting; rather it was the result of Saddam's lack of attention to maintenance—this applied especially to the electricity sector—and looting that came after the initial fighting was over.

The conflict had damaged telecommunications, the port of Umm Qasr, several highway bridges and more than a few buildings, but not much more.

"I have seen the enemy and he is us."—Pogo cartoon

Rumors about the replacement of General Garner as head of ORHA proved to be true. The new man, Paul "Jerry" Bremer—I will refer to him as the "Viceroy" as that was how he came to be referred to internally and that is how many of us felt he comported himself—soon arrived. He and Jay Garner overlapped in the Palace for several days, both accompanied by what seemed to be the strangeness of competing entourages, and then Jay was gone.

ORHA was gone too—name soon changed to CPA (Coalition Provisional Authority) to better represent that we were a coalition of allied partners—not just the US and the "Provisional" part meaning, we anticipated that our organization would soon be replaced by Iraqis. Or so we hoped.

The "coalition" part was certainly accurate—in the Palace we now had Brits, Australians, Spanish and Japanese, among others. Polish, Italian and other nations' troops were in other parts of Iraq and we saw their representatives in the Palace as well.

CPA started streaming in their own new personnel and the new

US people seemed to be arriving willy-nilly from God knows where. We were learning to speak in military lingo and that situation would have been described as "I had no visibility about that." I still never quite got what "the long pole in the tent" meant and what they meant at every meeting's end by "Are there any more alibis"? Alibis? I thought alibis were excuses, but surely that was not what they meant...

There was another colorful military term appropriate to CPA in my view and that was a two word military term that started with the word "cluster" and went on from there. The "cluster" word seemed increasingly to apply to many aspects of CPA's operations—from contracting, personnel, communications, coordination and decision making.

The Viceroy probably made some fifty significant decisions a day—these were called CPA Orders and maybe thirty-five or so of those were correct or at least defensible, but that left some that were outright doozies.

The most egregious was, in my view and in the view of many, the dissolving of the Iraqi Army, which I heard about one morning from the Viceroy at our 6:00 a.m. staff meeting. My reaction was one of incredulity: What? What? What?

So much for Garner's plan to keep these guys on the payroll and let them help rebuild Iraq. In one stroke, the Viceroy and his advisor—a former Clinton-era DOD official—had made a million plus men into unpaid and often desperate enemies. And by the way, they were armed!

Not much explanation was made that I heard beyond, "The Iraqi Army has already dissolved itself and better to start over with an entirely new force." What? What?

No, you get on the radio and tell the Army that everyone under a certain rank would be welcomed back—with appropriate vetting of course—be paid and reintegrated into a reformed Iraqi force. This reconstituted group would be a force against terrorism and other threats, and along with a reformed police force provide internal order, cooperate with coalition forces who would make it clear that their presence was temporary, and authority would be passed as soon as possible back to where it belonged, with the Iraqis.

Instead, the Viceroy decided otherwise, and automatically created an anti-coalition force that would morph into resistance fighters themselves, cost coalition lives and delay the conditions that would allow us to depart sooner as opposed to later.

The Viceroy's advisor—the former Pentagon official under Clinton—was the supposed author of this decision (we heard too that this was the Viceroy's final decision and was not vetted or approved in advance by USG in Washington by authorities up to and including the President). The advisor next went to Erbil in the Kurdish region and told CPA leadership there to go the next step and abolish the Kurd's military force, the Peshmerga!

Anyone with the slightest knowledge of the Kurds recent history, including Saddam's genocide against them post Gulf War I, would have immediately recognized that such an intention was beyond preposterous and would have been immediately and vehemently rejected by the Kurds had they ever gotten wind of it.

The head of CPA/Erbil was a friend, and I got the story directly from him. His reaction to the order to abolish the Peshmerga was a quick, "Yeah, we'll be sure and do that…"

Needless to say, and thankfully, that did not happen.

"We have seen the enemy and he is us."—Pogo cartoon

Speaking of the Viceroy, soon after his arrival we traveled together to Umm Qasr to rededicate the port post-repairs and also greet numerous, happy Iraqi dock workers who were back on the job. It already was a far cry from the damaged scene I had observed a few months earlier.

One of the first things we had Bechtel do, once conditions permitted, was to bring in a dredger from the UAE to clear the harbor of excess silt. Given Umm Qasr is at the confluence of the Tigris and Euphrates rivers on the Gulf, silt deposits in the harbor had to be constantly removed. If not, ships would have to unload offshore via tenders, adding much additional time and expense to the process.

This was vital to solve quickly, because had there been a humanitarian crisis post-invasion—which there wasn't, it turned out—there would have been added suffering among the Iraqis. Bechtel delivered, the harbor was dredged and ships began unloading at the docks.

However much progress was made every day, the Viceroy never seemed to be satisfied. At our daily senior staff meetings, I usually mentioned some task or project that Bechtel was implementing, which was invariably met with criticism of some sort from the Viceroy. So, despite a growing list of achievements in water, sewage, water conveyance, power generation, community-based programs, school rehabilitation and so forth, I started to tell the Viceroy nothing at staff meetings, as I suspected others did too. We included everything in daily reports to Washington, and it was all online anyway, and most senior managers simply grew tired of being yelled at by the Viceroy.

However unpleasant that kind of interaction with the Viceroy became, the worst was when he would launch into his "I have a letter from the president that says I can do anything with the Iraq reconstruction budget that I choose to do" speech. This diatribe happened frequently. My Deputy Chris and I took it on the chin for the team on these occasions.

To several ongoing programs underway, the Viceroy somehow took a dislike. We had been working on these programs for months, they had been awarded following proper procurement and contracting regulations, and staff and equipment had been deployed, yet the Viceroy was threatening to tear it all up and start over.

One day's pithy quip: "I am going to take all your money from X-project and pass the money out in the streets of al Hillah." If that had happened, all hell would have broken out legally and a good number of the twelve former USAID Mission Directors I had on the staff running programs would have resigned en mass.

In the alleged POTUS letter—if it actually existed—I don't believe that the Viceroy was being told to break the law by ignoring required competition, procurement and contracting rules. I was a risk-taker but not a law-breaker. My refusals, or at least my strong arguments to counter the Viceroy, made for a heavy load that tumbled down the food chain and affected morale. We didn't give in and the most egregious threats, thankfully, were not acted upon. A fifteen-minute pre-deployment briefing on procurement, contracting and grants made to the Viceroy in Washington, DC, would have avoided this issue entirely. Remember Pogo.

I was fortunate to have two wonderful deputies in Iraq. One concentrated on Mission related programs and operations, not the least of which was security for all our personnel who were by now fully present in Baghdad and, especially after the abolition of the Iraqi Army, under increased threat from them and other anti-coalition forces. Earl and I had solemnly sworn that we would do everything in our power to keep our personnel safe.

We had a robust security force by now and we estimated that our expenses, with an additional security presence, was costing us twenty-five percent of our entire Iraq operation. This was not what we had originally planned. We were blessed and plain lucky that none of our direct mission, NGO and contractor personnel—numbering well over 600 by now—were killed or wounded during our tenure in Iraq.

The other Deputy, Chris, had the unenviable but necessary job of being our primary liaison with CPA. Given the example above, this was a hard, exhausting job, but Chris was tireless and determined, and time after time pulled victory out of the jaws of defeat.

Part of our problem was that some of CPA's upper echelons were not favorably disposed to us given past Agency grievances else-where—the Viceroy from his days in Malawi as a junior FSO, and one of his principal deputies from a posting to Egypt.

Chris and I worked every day to convince these people and others that our agency was doing exactly the kind of work we had been doing for decades overseas—economic development and reconstruc-tion—albeit here and now at a level and complexity we had never seen elsewhere. We were a valuable and essential tool in the toolbox.

We also were confronted by hosts of mostly well-meaning military colleagues who had never heard of our agency, had no idea what we did, and had no clue why we had financing, especially if they did not. This military group tended to rotate out of Iraq every ninety days or so, meaning that by the time we had convinced and somewhat converted them to understanding how we worked and our worth, they were gone, leaving us to start over with an entirely new group.

Many lessons of "civ/mil cooperation" were learned by all sides as a result of Iraq. We were soon espousing the importance of the "three-legged stool" of defense, diplomacy and development.

Or as I used to say and lament—Kumbaya hat firmly in place—we are all on the same side, right? It is better to work together than to work against each other. Easy, right?

Sometimes Pogo's wise words echoed loudly—too loudly—in my ear.

The security situation kept us constantly on our toes, and it was clear that when we got rocketed or shelled, the insurgents were trying to hurt us. We were very busy and focused on work, but one could never forget to abide by security rules. We liked and respected our contract guard force, mostly young Brits and veterans of the SAS. They were professional and kept the Rambo stuff to a minimum.

Our offices were mostly located in the "Convention Center" across the road from the Al-Rashid Hotels. Earl and I had modest corner offices with a thick plastic sheet for a wall replacing the former glass windows that had been shattered in earlier fighting. Our technicians worked hard to install our computer equipment that provided us connectivity to communicate with our colleagues in the Green Zone as well as Washington.

One day one of my local Iraq female hires came into the office to say how much she appreciated the job with USAID as it provided her family with a means of support and the hope for a better future. "By the way," she added, "I am Jewish, and my family is one of the few remaining Jewish families left in Baghdad." She said that in order to protect their lives, they could not admit to anyone their true religion and asked me to swear silence. I told her that her secret was safe with me. I wish I now knew her and her family's ultimate fate.

About noon every day, there was a controlled explosion of excess ordinance from somewhere in the Green Zone. We normally were too busy to keep track of the time, and when the huge explosion would go off at noon, we were usually shocked and even fell beside our desks to take cover. Earl and I would look at our watches, shake our heads, and get back to work.

––––––––––––

Many of us moved quarters several times as CPA grew and its components settled into more permanent work and living spaces. For a while we were in thin-skinned trailers near the bank of the Tigris and near the site of the eventual new US Embassy.

One night, a particularly severe outbreak of shooting erupted on the other side of the river. A recently arrived contingent of very attentive US Marines took the shooting to be an attack and quickly returned fire—all this happening around us as we *ducked and covered*.

This time the actual cause of the gunfire was due to a soccer match that the Iraqis had won. Like other gunfire, celebratory gunfire eventually returns to earth, sometimes with disastrous consequences. After several bangs and pings on my trailer roof, our security guys hustled us into a hardened shelter to wait for the celebration to die down.

Other times we would hear Green Zone security alarms but would have no more information. Were rockets on the way? Had the Green Zone been breached by insurgents? We tried to think fast and get our staff to shelter as quickly as possible.

Several times I pulled out my cell phone and called my wife in Austin. "Turn on cable news and let me know what's going on." She would then report to me and I would report what she had found to our security folks on the ground.

"Duck and cover" became part of our new reality—whether coming from our security personnel in tense situations or eventually as part of the security loud-speakers that came to ring the Green Zone. It was also to be part of every Embassy's security drills where I would subsequently serve post-Iraq.

"Duck and cover. Duck and cover. Get away from the windows," would be the security drill run by the Marine Security Guards worldwide. The pre-recorded male voice became very familiar.

Final note: The "Duck and Cover" became the name of eventual Embassy pubs in both Afghanistan and Iraq, though for me in Iraq that came later when an actual Embassy was opened.

Notwithstanding our precautions, we had a number of close calls, security-wise. Once we had a huge truck bomb go off at one Green Zone entrance a quarter mile away that shook the entire Palace and rattled the windows in the middle of a CPA senior staff meeting chaired by the Viceroy.

Incoming rocket fire shook the ground occasionally—once when our boss Andrew was in town from DC—two Brits working for us came close to being hit by incoming rocket fire right after an otherwise short and nice office Thanksgiving celebration and then, oh yes, there was that time they attacked our hotel with a trailer full of rockets, but that comes a bit later.

As reconstruction work progressed, we, led by Becthtel, were making progress getting schools repaired in time for the opening of the school year. I had surveyed damaged and ruined schools before and now was starting to see repaired ones.

One little glitch came about when a top security advisor from the White House decided to visit and see the progress for herself. I wasn't in Baghdad at the time but the reports started coming into us that the advisor was not happy as a result of her visit.

What had happened? A little digging showed that she had visited a couple of the repaired schools and had provided the kids and teachers some photos from Washington: photos of President Bush shot from the rear as he walked Barney, the black Scottish terrier owned by 43. Other photos were of Barney alone.

Apparently, the kids and teachers had recoiled in something like horror. The problem was that to many of the poorer Shia kids in the schools she visited, dogs in general were considered "haram", unclean or forbidden, and a black dog was considered especially bad. On top of that to show a photo of POTUS from the rear was also considered very bad form and culturally inappropriate.

For that, the White House was questioning, we were told, the effectiveness of our overall school repair and reconsideration program.

I got on the phone, explained what had happened to Andrew and he made a short trek to the White House to explain how a few well-meaning acts by the advisor had been a serious cultural faux pas in the eyes of the Iraqis. Andrew explained it in full, and we were told that the advisor's reaction was a resigned "Oh....", but at least we were off the hook.

I got out of the Green Zone as much as possible as I needed to travel Iraq to see our projects in person, deal with contractors, NGOs and government officials. I had no desire to be a "Prisoner of the Green Zone."

My boss Andrew came to visit a couple of times and since he was a big shot, he came with his own plane. We went first to Erbil to meet with the Kurds who understandably saw what we were doing in Federal Iraq and wanted more assistance. We told them that the house further south was on fire and therefore they needed most of the attention. We would do what we could in Kurdistan but they were only suffering smoke damage.

Andrew and I had the opportunity to meet with a number of Kurdish widows and other survivors of the "Anfal" campaign, Saddam's genocide against the Kurds after Gulf War I that killed some 180,000 Kurds. Some had even survived the poison gas attack that Saddam had carried out on Halabja in 1988.

We then flew to the south to observe more of our projects there, even entering into the domain of the 'Marsh Arabs', as they were called. Water flowing from the south-flowing Tigris and Euphrates had formed this unique ecological zone where many of the inhabitants lived in arch-shaped reed huts. The health and hunger situation, especially for small children, seemed acute.

Saddam had dammed a large portion of the marshes and much of it had dried up leaving the Marsh Arabs with an even more tenuous situation than before. There was a lot of academic hand-wringing about the fate of the marshes in the post-Saddam days until a determined Iraqi with a bagful of dynamite blew up most of the small impoundment dams. It would take a while but it seemed that the marshes were well on their way to being marshes again.

Andrew and I were followed around during this period by a US television crew from C-Span who recorded our every move and word that would be broadcast later on TV in the US.

We were not far at this point from Samara, near to the site of some of Saddam's "mass graves" where Saddam had driven thousands of innocent Kurds and Shia into trenches, killing them or burying them alive. For this foray, a reporter from the *Washington Post* accompanied us. He had told us his last activity prior to leaving for Iraq was to march in an anti-Iraq war demonstration in DC.

As we looked out over hectares of ground in from of us, we observed the remains of mass murder and the flotsam left in its wake—bones protruding from the ground, broken flip flops, soil covered clothes, pieces of plastic bags flapping in the wind.

Whatever one thought about the Iraq War, I for one was glad Saddam was not around anymore to kill his own people. I don't know if the *Washington Post* reporter's mind was changed, and it didn't matter, but one only had to be human to feel the suffering of the poor innocent Kurds and Shia who had been on Saddam's lists and had ended up here.

When Andrew and I returned to Baghdad, we had dinner with the UN head in Iraq, Brazilian diplomat Sergio Viera de Mello. Distinguished and soft spoken, de Mello and Andrew compared plans for Iraq and discussed joint US-UN programs. How fortunate we were to have such a good counterpart.

Two days later, I was in a meeting with the Viceroy that included my Texas Senator Kay Bailey Hutchison. We had just begun the meeting when a distant but huge explosion shook the Palace and our meeting room.

We found out quickly what had transpired. A truck bomb laden with explosives had made its way past security barriers at the UN offices a few miles away and had blown up the entire compound. Sadly, Sergio was among the many UN fatalities that day, some of whom I had known and worked with in Kuwait. I visited the blast site the next day and surveyed the damage and tragic results up close.

The enemy was not shooting blanks and casualties were starting to mount. A future UN friend, who was on Sergio's senior staff and had been in the UN building at the time of the blast, told me she was saved because she had dropped a document on the floor at the exact moment of the blast, and when she bent over to pick it up, she had been shielded by a heavy safe and cabinets, thus avoiding the full force of the explosion.

I went by the UN building ruins the next day and was immediately met by that horrible smell that I came to know well in Haiti after the 2010 earthquake. I told myself at the time it was the rotting food from the UN cafeteria left in the hot sun, but I think I knew better and full well what that smell was.

My next trip outside Baghdad was to Hillah, south of the capital and the site of the ruins of Babylon. CPA had a regional office there, and we in USAID had a rep there too—an old friend—and it was time for me to make the rounds to inspect projects and meet and greet locals.

Traveling by FAV to Hillah also represented my most ill-advised moment in Iraq—I drove there alone. Fortunately, there was no problem, and coming back, I was part of a large and very well-armed convoy.

Walking through the ruins of Babylon was awe inspiring. My guide, the Governor, pointed out that this was where Prophet Ezekiel had walked after the conquest of Jerusalem and Babylonia exile in 598 BC. A room off the main palace, he told me, was where Alexander the Great had died in 323 BC at the age of thirty-two.

True to form, Saddam had undertaken a renovation of some of the ancient Babylonian walls—surely to the horror of archaeologists everywhere—and inserting new bricks in the walls with his name on them. He had even had a canal dug around the ruins further damaging one of the world's greatest ancient treasures.

The governor leaned down, picked up a block carved with cuneiform script and laid it in my hands. This was at a minimum from 500 BC. There were thousands of such blocks lying around in the ruins that stretched far into the distance.

I had to travel a few times outside Iraq—one to a Mission Directors conference in DC, once to Amman to coordinate some matters with USAID and State there, and once for a medical matter also to Amman. By this time my Agency had hired the services of a humanitarian NGO and their nineteen-seat prop plane to fly in NGO staff that otherwise would have had a far more difficult time entering Iraq.

Our direct USAID staff, of course, got to use the plane since we were paying for it—but the truth was that we had to keep the existence of the plane under wraps because there was no doubt that CPA would have monopolized its use.

Using the plane was always a thrill: due to the threat of Surface to Air missiles (SAMs), the plane would fly upwards in a tight corkscrew until reaching 20,000 feet, where it would level off and proceed to Amman. Coming back to Baghdad was the same in reverse—a tight corkscrew down. On the way down, an automated voice recording from the cockpit could be heard announcing, "Pull up, pull up, pull up."

I think that was considered normal as we always landed safely. The pilots were white South Africans who seemed to be having the time of their lives (was that delighted laughing I was hearing from the cockpit?) as corkscrew landings and takeoffs were hardly normal flying. They explained to me, "In the Angolan war, the rebels shot SAMs at us all the time, but the corkscrew meant they could never lock on."

One takeoff, about halfway to 20,000 feet, I thought I saw a SAM flash by outside my window moving straight upward as we merrily corkscrewed skyward. I don't know if I really saw it or not, as I mostly concentrated on making it to 20,000 feet and then a nice glide into the well familiar and peaceful territory of Amman.

When I eventually made my move into the Al Rashid Hotel, I would throw back the curtains at 5:30 a.m. just as the sun was coming up and look out over Saddam's massive parade ground with two crossed huge metal swords emerging from the ground. The hands holding the swords were supposedly modeled on Saddam's own hands. Iranian helmets left from dead Iranians from the Iran-Iraq war were embedded in the monument too, as yet another tasteful, artful touch. I would look out at the parade ground as the sun rose over Baghdad and mutter to myself, "No rockets today."

Until there were...

I was on a US military jet flying back to Baghdad from an Iraq donors' conference in Madrid, Spain, with a contingent of other CPA people. Once we landed, we started hearing the news that the Al-Rashid was under attack.

The Al-Rashid Hotel was the Green Zone hotel where "bombs over Baghdad" had been broadcast at the start of Gulf War I, and until our troops had taken it over in April, had a mosaic of the face of Bush 41 that one was obliged to walk over as he entered the hotel.

Moving our staff to the Al-Rashid was my fifth or sixth move in the Green Zone. I looked forward to what I hoped would be an improved living environment for our entire staff.

The road beside the Al-Rashid had just been opened by CPA to outside traffic and the insurgents took little time to take advantage and strike. As the sun rose, they pulled up a trailer full of rockets beside the hotel and proceeded to blast away at my side of the hotel, rockets hitting various floors on the north side. In one case, a rocket crashed through the window and lodged without detonating in the wall above someone's headboard as they slept.

CPA staff spread over the nine stories of the Al-Rashid made their way in various stages of dress or undress to the stairwells, at times dragging themselves on their hands and knees over broken glass in an attempt to escape.

Worst of all, a rocket had made a direct hit on my floor that killed a soldier two rooms over from my own as he blasted away at the trailer with his weapon. We mourned his loss but I was at the same time grateful that our USAID staff had otherwise suffered only cuts and bruises.

There was one more important international meeting that took place among donor friends of Iraq to help with planning and support for Iraq after the first phase of work was done. This conference was held in my old stomping grounds of Jordan at a resort on the Dead Sea where the temperatures were not for the faint of heart and often surpassed 110 degrees Farenheit in summer.

One of my former Jordanian government colleagues by the name of Bassam was running the show for the Jordanians. He seemed mightily worried as the heat was beating down and starting to overcome the ACs that were supposed to be cooling the large tent where the plenary sessions were held.

VIPs were everywhere: Prime Ministers, Secretary of State Colin Powell, a bevy of Congress people, and other notables from across the Middle East, Europe and North America.

As I walked down the stairs at the resort I noticed a familiar face walking up the stairs. It was Shimon Peres, the President of Israel. We were introduced and Peres was told that I was in charge of much of the US "Iraq Reconstruction" effort. President Peres wanted to talk, and his message was the clear question he posed: "How can Israel be involved to help the reconstruction effort in Iraq?"

I made my excuses and left the conversation without being impolite and did my best to avoid President Peres for the rest of the day. When I returned to the JW Marriott Hotel in Amman that evening, there were two yellow telephone messages waiting for me: "Please call Shimon Peres urgently." Every instinct I had told me that this was a call I had no business returning.

Back in Baghdad, I reported the encounter to my colleague Ambassador Ryan Crocker—future Ambassador to both Iraq and Afghanistan—and a true Middle East stalwart for the US.

I didn't have to explain to Ryan why I didn't call Peres back. We were already being accused of starting a war for the sake of Iraq's oil—completely untrue, of course—but the last thing we needed was to be accused of prosecuting the war for the benefit of Israel, even if they only wanted to help. "No way," I said, and Ryan backed me up. He also sent a cable to Washington describing the chain of events, and I fortunately never heard another word about it.

To list USAID's accomplishments in Iraq during my tenure there is inconsistent with the style of this book, but I think essential to an even partial telling of the tale. There was tremendous progress made under "warlike conditions" as we refer to it, and the story is rarely, if ever, mentioned and appreciated by the US public.

We tried (and tried) to get the word out but often did not succeed for various reasons: the US press was less interested in good news than in the latest bad news; "accomplishments in Iraq" was not part of what came to be the overall narrative about Iraq, especially in subsequent years and Administrations; and our reporting was full of detailed information than made many "normal" peoples' eyes glaze over.

However, I think it is important to get the word out even if I do it now years later and somewhat out of frustration. Iraqi colleagues were by the way, in large part, a hard-working and talented group, and the accomplishments listed below are theirs as much as anyone's.

There were and are thousands of successes that should be mentioned and hopefully appreciated. USAID's partners—US and Iraqi contractors, NGOs, the US Army Corps of Engineers, and especially hard-working Iraqis, were essential parts of these achievements.

For example, one of the great unknown stories of "Iraq reconstruction" is the tale of how the old (Saddam era) Iraq currency was completely replaced and old currency gathered up and destroyed.

In 2003, USAID partner Bearing Point was awarded a large contract to help strengthen the Iraqi economy. The myriad of activities included building a commercial banking network, SOE (State Enterprise) reform, improve the interbank data transfer, strengthen the oil for food program, commercial law reform, developing trade policy regulations, microfinance and SME loan programs as well as the collection, and verification of existing currency with the subsequent printing and distribution of a new Iraqi currency.

The justification for replacing the currency was threefold. First, the new bills would no longer contain the face of Saddam Hussein. Second, there were concerns that a high-volume of Iraqi notes were counterfeit, especially the 10,000 Saddam Dinar which was not traded at face value and holders were only able to obtain seventy percent of its value, and finally, there were two currencies in operation, the Iraqi Dinar and the Swiss Franc which was used in the Kurdish area. The new Iraqi Dinar would replace both existing currencies.

Bearing Point's involvement in the Iraqi Dinar currency exchange was the most opaque activity under their economic growth contract. This was intentional as information was provided only on a need to know basis. The "war room" where operational activities took place had a secure access and only authorized individuals were permitted to enter.

Bearing Point was working with several institutions under this operation, specifically, with British officials who were responsible for the production and off-site storage of the new Iraqi Dinars. The location of these facilities were in undisclosed cities in Europe.

US Treasury officials were part of the team as they were working closely as the "shadow" Central Bank. Their role was to develop the framework for an autonomous entity that would no longer be subject to the control of the political regime.

The US military was responsible for the secure collection of old Iraqi notes as well as the distribution of the new Iraqi notes. Armored Humvees and their military escorts which included mounted 50 caliber machine guns were the "Brink's" convoy.

The oddest activity, but one which is probably still in operation today, was the physical inspection of every note. This was the agreed process whereby human inspectors manually checked each and every note to determine if the note was counterfeit. The bank received an equivalent new note if it was legitimate. If the note was fake, it was shredded and burned. The secret warehouse where the currency was held contained several trillion Iraqi notes. It was excellent planning or a miracle or both that the entire nation's currency was completely replaced without any deaths or theft of new currency.

This story is largely unknown outside Iraq but another one where our combined efforts—especially Iraqi—had a tremendous positive effect.

I guarantee that most informed Americans, and even other USAID people elsewhere in the world, have little to no idea of what was accomplished in Iraq. Our communications staff sent out notices every day with progress updates but the US press was not interested in positive news. I gave interview after interview but it never seemed to matter.

I flew home briefly to Texas for my oldest daughter's college graduation and saw it for myself: our efforts at reconstruction were being painted as a failure in the making. The press refused to be diverted in their negative narrative despite all the evidence to the contrary.

I refuse to completely let it go and even years later, and want to tell the story one more time with the hope that the work and accomplishments of many will be finally noted and perhaps even appreciated. So this is the real story below and in Annex 2.

USAID's programs in the early reconstruction phase in Iraq concentrated on four strategic areas: restoring essential infrastructure; supporting essential health and education; expanding economic opportunity; and improving Iraqi government accountability and efficiency.

The detailed accomplishments listed in Annex 2 correspond to the first year of work only, from April 2003 when we first arrived in Baghdad through March 2004, a period of one year.

The achievements listed in the Annex—and obviously there were many of them in this particular one-year period and which continued a few years more with high-level funding prior to diminishing, as it should have—was the result of many actors: first the American people who provided the funds; USAID itself and its scores of dedicated contractors and NGO partners; other parts of CPA; international organizations and especially the scores of patriotic Iraqis who were our boots on the ground and carried on in the face of danger and death threats.

The work was carried out often in hostile and "warlike" conditions.

When the foreigners had to hunker down or "duck and cover" it was most often the Iraqi employees who did the heavy lifting, often risking their lives to get the job done. I will always see the prospects of a rewarding future for these Iraqis—clever, hardworking, brave and dependable—who were key to most of our efforts.

Final note: When the Viceroy wrote his own book about his year in Iraq, many of the accomplishments he cited were those I have cited and led and were carried out by USAID. The truth is that he was not particularly supportive of most of these programs while they were being planned and implemented but more than happy to claim credit for them at the end.

Much was going on back on the CPA front. The Viceroy was finally told in no uncertain terms back in DC to accelerate the transition back to Iraqi control so many works were underway—a new constitution, election planning, full Ministerial turnovers and scores of other initiatives that we had little visibility of but that were essential to getting Iraqis back in control of Iraq.

I was also filling out paperwork as I was told that I was to be nominated as a US Ambassador and had to be fully vetted again, a new security clearance would be needed, and all past speeches and remarks made available and added to the vast paperwork pile.

It was Andrew who ultimately asked me if I wanted to pursue this step, and after all that had come before, I guess the answer was at least a resounding "Why not?" The notion of continuing to serve in the Foreign Service post-Iraq was appealing, and being an Ambassador—while I had never sought such "glory"—(USAID workers didn't get offered many Ambassadorships) it was an honor. I conferred with my spouse and we said yes.

I departed Iraq after sixteen months in theatre, thoroughly exhausted but overall pleased with our many achievements. The staff gave me a huge going away party with a few embarrassingly large pictures of me on the wall.

Joy had previously sent me, for no apparent reason, three fake pink plastic flamingos that I had put in front of my latest Green Zone residence as a sign of pure kitsch and I don't know what else.

I made heartfelt goodbye remarks to the troops and then made a gift of the flamingos to Earl and Chris. I told the Iraqis in attendance that to explain the significance of three pink flamingos was for me a cultural "bridge too far" but to please ask Chris all about it later.

Iraqi employees gave me a framed metal plaque with words about my "leadership of the first ever USAID Mission to Iraq—USAIDs largest program in history. Together we have made history". The plaque had engravings of great Iraqi historical figures like Hammurabi and the iconic female figure of Kahramanh, a symbol of modernity.

But looking at the engraving of Hammurabi speaking with an ancient scribe holding a tablet, I recalled the words of more than a few Iraqis I had met over the course of the past year, "You know, sir, we *did* invent laws and writing."

Lest we forget.

Swaziland (Eswatini)

To BECOME A CONFIRMED Ambassador, one has to jump through hoops and the process is not for the faint of heart. Naturally, it beats getting rocketed in the Green Zone, but there were scores of forms to fill out, clearances to obtain, new people to meet and a required move back to Washington, DC.

I had tried to avoid serving in DC as much as possible in the past, and every time it had looked like I would have no recourse, my plans would be changed. I had been lucky to this point but between being nominated by POTUS as Ambassador and being confirmed and departing for post, there was often at least a six-month wait and, if you or your country was somehow controversial with Congress, the wait could be longer or your nomination could go nowhere at all.

There was little chance that a nominee for little Swaziland would be too controversial so I just had the normal clearances to deal with. The State Department provided me a couple good junior FSOs in the Africa Bureau to assist me.

Moving to DC was again a solitary affair as the family was established in Texas but at least we could easily connect. No one was shooting at me this time either, so it was not too hard to get through the process.

Soon after being back, however, I found myself scouring DC traffic circles for attackers and IEDs. On one weekend trip to rural Maryland with a friend, a fire alarm went off in the distance. I excitedly told my friend that we had to take cover—now! As an ex Viet Nam helicopter pilot, he assured me that there was nothing to worry about. Besides, I didn't want to jump into a wet Maryland ditch anyway. Then, in the old State Department building, the heaters would come on with a bang and a shudder and I would have to force myself not to hit the deck.

I was not like this in Iraq. We were too busy, and more importantly, there were people counting on me to be an example, to be a leader and to be strong.

I guess this was my version of PTSD. Many who had been in far more dangerous situations than I would experience PTSD much worse. Still, it was real, and one had to deal with it, but for me it passed rapidly.

I spent six months meeting with people on the Hill—Texas Senator Cornyn asked for a briefing on Iraq reconstruction—and especially those who knew or cared about Swaziland. Meanwhile, I waited for my clearances to come through and for my confirmation hearing to be scheduled.

I asked the Foreign Service Institute if they could arrange for Siswati lessons for me—English was the working language, but Siswati was the spoken one. It seemed to be a considerate thing for the US Ambassador to be able to make greetings in the local language, and FSI accommodated me.

It didn't take me too long to figure out this was going to be a lot harder than learning, say, Spanish, but I persevered for a month, had a good teacher and learned enough to demonstrate I had at least tried to learn it. Otherwise said, I was learning just enough to get into trouble.

Next there was a required Ambassadorial training session we all did with spouses—we called it "Charm School"—so Joy came to DC for that.

"What happens," she asked, "if I fail Charm School?" I didn't know the answer to that.

I eventually had my Senate sub-committee hearing with two other Ambassadors-designate for Africa. I had gone to grad school with one of them long ago and had gotten to know the other one and his spouse during Charm School. The latter, Joe and his wife Kathleen, had nearly been hostages in Iran after the Embassy takeover there in 1979 and had taken refuge in the Canadian Ambassador's residence until they and colleagues could be spirited out of Teheran by the CIA. Ref the movie *Argo*.

Long story short: we had our hearing, a couple of Senators showed up, we answered questions, no one made any embarrassing mistakes and we all were confirmed.

I was actually introduced to the Committee by both of my Texas Senators, which was not normal and a great honor. I knew one of them from Baghdad and the other, Senator Cornyn, I knew from the briefing on Iraq reconstruction he requested.

We were set to go—almost.

It is considered bad form to pack your effects, rent out your house and so forth until you are actually confirmed. But once you have the confirmation, you need to get your logistics squared away and get moving. Thus, Joy was back in Austin packing us out and trying to rent the house.

I was fortunate this time as Joy decided to join me for at least the first year, and our son—going into tenth grade—was also willing, not happy, but willing to come too.

I called her one afternoon to ask how renting the house looked. "Not so good," she said. "No serious takers yet, but by the way, what is this Dr. Pepper bottle I found in the garage that you have marked, 'Holy Water blessed by Pope John Paul II?'"

I reminded her that this water was given to us in Jordan in 2000 by a Jordanian Christian employee when John Paul II had come to dedicate the baptismal site of Christ at "Bethany beyond the Jordan". The bottle had been forgotten, unseen and unused in my garage ever since the family's return home.

"Look," I said, "sprinkle some of the Holy Water on the For Rent sign, a little on the house and lawn, and heck, maybe a few drops on yourself. It can't hurt."

She called me back three hours later. "You won't believe what just happened."

"You rented the house?" I asked.

"Yes", she said, "but you won't believe *who* rented it. The Catholic Diocese of Austin! Three priests are moving in next week."

When I was sworn in on the State Department's snazzy seventh floor, there was a distinguished and diverse crowd of long-time friends, family and colleagues in attendance. The contingent of Carolina folks did not know the larger groups of Texans, and it was fun to see them interact and hit it off. Old friends of my parents came from my original hometown to represent my deceased parents. Agency head Andrew was there too, and I enjoyed introducing him to my Texas father-in-law who had deep political roots in Texas just as Andrew had his original political roots in Massachusetts. Chris and Earl and a smattering of other Iraq buddies were there too.

I recalled my father-in-law's question to me from long ago about why I couldn't get a "real job" in Texas versus taking their daughter off to West Africa.

"George, does this count as a real job?" I asked him. He was non-committal but I decided to take that as at least a "maybe".

Swaziland was certainly not the diplomatic center of the universe and I had understood that from the start. The real challenge in Swaziland was HIV/AIDS and how to forge the most effective programs possible to counter the outbreak.

I didn't know much about Swaziland at this point, but I was acutely aware that they had the highest HIV/AIDS rate in the world. A quick look at the mission's HIV/AIDS programs showed a mishmash of small programs that seemed to me to lack coherence based on a sound strategy. That would be my main focus for the length of my stay there.

Literally on the way out the door, the Assistant Secretary for Africa, herself an ex-USAID person, whispered in my ear that there was ten million dollars in an account in the US that had been left over from a Swaziland USAID project that for some reason had been curtailed. Figure out how to effectively program that money in Swaziland, she said, and you can use it.

That was great news. Ten million wasn't so significant for something like "Iraq Reconstruction" but it was a big deal for little Swaziland, which was off the beaten track and for which budgets were always tight.

So with spouse and son, we departed the US once again for our posting in southern Africa. The flight was more than eighteen hours just to fly from Atlanta to Johannesburg, where my new driver had come to drive us the rest of the way.

The US Ambassador to South Africa received me at the Embassy and offered every courtesy. The Marine guards saluted her which I thought was pretty cool. Alas, I knew that Swaziland had yet to have Marine Guards and in fact the little Embassy was on two top floors of the Central Bank building, but an Embassy nonetheless.

Jeffrey, the official Ambassador's driver, drove us the three and half hours from Pretoria to Mbabane, the capital and our new home. It seemed to be a beautiful country from what I was seeing so far.

In order to officially begin one's work as an Ambassador anywhere in the world, the Ambassador-designate must present his or her credentials to the Head of State. When it came time to present my credentials to the King, my party made its way down the mountain from Mbabane to the palace a few miles away. The King, Mswati II, was there to meet me dressed in traditional robes. We proceeded to inspect a contingent of Swazi military while the band played the "Star Bangled Banner".

Inspecting troops with a King was a first for me.

I presented my letters of credential to the King ("His Majesty")—I was used to the name from Jordan days—then made short remarks followed by the King's own remarks.

I had heard from other Ambassadors that King Mswati's father, King Mabuza I, had obliged credential-presenting Ambassadors to approach him on hands and knees. I was very glad that custom had gone away.

Our parties proceeded from the first palace room to a bigger and longer Throne Room where the King, appropriately enough, sat on an ornate chair (a throne?) while motioning me to another ornate chair beside him. Our little party of Americans from the Embassy sat backs to the wall looking across the room at the royal Swazi party, dressed in red and black traditional cloth robes, with sandals and the rest of their traditional regalia. Their backs were similarly against the other wall.

Both parties stared at each other for a while in complete silence. It had all the ingredients of an awkward stare-off and I wasn't exactly sure if I should try to break the awkwardness or keep my silence.

I decided to open my big mouth.

"Your Majesty, I wanted to tell you that before coming to Swaziland, I took a whole month of Siswati language lessons and can do all the clicks in Siswati."

The King looked at me amused and said, "Let's hear it!"

I proceeded to utter a likely close approximation of the Siswaiti clicks for the benefit of all. The Swazis, including the King, broke into gales of laughter, clapping their hands, seemingly pleased about this new development in the meeting.

Awkwardness had disappeared, so we chatted amiably for a while and eventually we took our leave, found our way back to our vehicles and back up the big hill to Mbabane.

I had learned that the appropriate and strategic use of humor was generally a good thing. Most Africans I had met, and the Swazis were no exception, used humor themselves and seemed to normally appreciate it from foreigners. It broke down barriers and made everyone seem a little more human.

For me, the episode had evoked a warm reaction from the King and the rest of the Swazis and perhaps, most importantly, from then on I seemed to have little difficulty in getting appointments with the King or his close associates. Access was important.

Yes, this was the US talking and not Andorra (no offense to Andorra) and maybe that was most important, but I suspected that the positive impressions made at the credentialing ceremony also played a part.

When Swaziland was a British protectorate, they located the capital of Mbabane in the hills above the then malaria zone, so our climate was temperate and mild. It could also rain torrents when it did rain, accompanied by huge and constant bolts of lightning. The lightning was made worse, we were told, by the large metal content in the hills that surrounded us. All that rain rendered our part of Swaziland green and verdant most of the year as well. It seemed that God and the US Government had successfully conspired to place me as far away as possible from the heat, dust, deserts and dangers of Iraq. I was grateful to both.

I started to get out of the office and the capital as much as possible to see the countryside, meet the people, show the flag, give speeches to schools and civic organizations and get a feel for my new home, however temporary.

I especially loved visiting the kids in elementary and high schools, at HIV/AIDS events and even orphanages—the latter always a bittersweet experience. Invariably, the kids would be asked to sing for their guests and they did so with amazing harmony and beauty. In the US, I figured that ten percent of the people could carry a tune. In Swaziland, the percentage had to be ninety percent. Wonderful!

A look at the small but diverse anti-HIV/AIDS programs in our portfolio got my attention from the start. In my experience, programs worked best if they were fewer in number and larger in budget and based on a sound strategy. CDC soon provided us a full time advisor who helped considerably, and another US advisor who was attached to the Swazi HIV/AIDS agency was another welcome addition.

It turned out the latter advisor was one of the top specialists anywhere on the effect of male circumcision as a factor in lowering transmission. Male circumcision promotion programs were soon to be among the tools in the anti-HIV/AIDS toolbox.

Our timing was fortunate too in that US pharmaceutical giant Bristol Myers Squibb had pledged to build and finance an AIDS prevention and treatment clinic in Mbabane that would be staffed by US and local physicians.

Soon the construction of the clinic was underway—a welcome and visible example of US private investment in the fight against HIV/AIDS, Swaziland's biggest threat. A full thirty-three percent of the Swazi population of reproductive age was HIV-positive, the largest such percentage of any country on earth.

The HIV/AIDS situation was so dire that much of an entire generation had died from AIDS complications, leaving an upcoming generation of "AIDs orphans" who were cared for by grandparents or in a worst-case scenario were being raised by other children. We estimated that by the end of the decade, a full twelve percent of Swaziland's population would be made up of AIDS orphans.

There were many aspects to getting control of HIV—some of course cultural. The lack of "fidelity in marriage or other relationships", to put it delicately, was a major factor in Swaziland's high infection rate. Unfortunately, there was a long tradition of Swazis being anything but faithful to one partner. Too many people had multiple partners, and that of course served to proliferate the rate of HIV infection.

Another factor was "knowing one's status"—did you have HIV? Far too many Swazis rejected getting tested so the problem and infection rate continued to climb. With anti-retroviral medication becoming more and more available, being HIV-positive was no longer the death sentence it once was, but no ARVs could be made available absent a test to determine one's status in the first place.

When it came time to dedicate the Mbabane HIV/AIDS clinic that had been financed by Bristol Myers Squibb, I had the bright idea of asking the King, as part of the dedication ceremony for the clinic, if he and I could be "tested" in front of the TV cameras, setting a powerful example for "knowing one's status" to the Swazi public.

I knew that if this happened—no status results would have to be disclosed—many lives could potentially be saved. If it was okay for the King to be tested, then it was surely okay for the population in general to be tested.

I ran this idea past the King's advisors and was hopeful for a few days but then sadly the answer came back: No. I was disappointed at this lost opportunity.

———————

As previously stated, Swaziland was a physically beautiful place with small mountains, forests, game parks and even golf courses. Most of my previous countries had had plenty of sand traps but lacked the rest of the course. In Swaziland, there was a Gary Player-designed course not far down the hill from my residence, and I tried to take advantage of it when I could.

The only problem was when it started to rain—and rain in sheets amid an urgent siren that called out from the clubhouse. Thor would get to work on his lightning bolts falling around us every few seconds, and the only solution was to run like crazy (no golf carts in Swaziland) for the safety of the clubhouse.

There was also a troop of monkeys that awaited you on the second green. I thought they would likely steal the golf balls that landed near their turf but I actually don't think I ever lost a ball that way. Other ways, yes.

The real Swaziland, however, was not that of golf courses or game parks. The perks of South Africa—a paved road network, reliable electricity, cell phones, bank ATMs and shopping centers were there, but one only had to get off the main roads into the countryside and see how the regular Swazis lived to realize that poverty was real and to see all the accompanying problems that poverty wrought as well.

My wife had found a job with the World Food Program and soon she had even better insights into Swaziland's landscape of hunger and poverty than I had.

Having Joy and my son with me in Mbabane was a blessing while it lasted, but the experiment of taking our son was not working out. The local prep school's curriculum was not coinciding well with the US one he would need for university in the States, and we were not much impressed by the quality of education he was receiving anyway.

He had played both football and lacrosse back home, and it made us sad to see him walk the grounds of our residence twirling his lacrosse stick all alone. Lacrosse had not quite made it to southern Africa.

We sadly concluded that we needed to get him home and back to his former school before he'd lost too much time. When his sisters came to visit us over Christmas, he accompanied them back to Texas and moved in temporarily with his grandparents. Joy decided to complete the rest of the first year with me in Swaziland but knew she would have to move home too.

———————

There was a constant refrain in Swaziland extolling the importance of tradition and culture. The King's constant participation in cultural ceremonies was evidence of that as well as the populations' firm acceptance and pride in expressions of Swazi culture.

One of the best known examples of Swazi culture was the annual "Reed Dance" where thousands of unmarried and mostly topless Swazi "maidens" in traditional costumes danced and clapped their way around open fields before dignitaries seated in the stands above as the dancers passed them.

Someone asked my wife how many dancing maidens could be expected to perform each year at the Reed Dance. My spouse—certainly not me—made a somewhat typically irreverent answer: "You count the breasts and divide by two."

Principal among the dignitaries at the Reed Dance, of course, was the King. The King was supposed to review the latest crop of maidens, and if the notion struck him, become engaged to a lucky girl and put on King Mswati's fiancée list. I could never quite determine how many of those there were, but it was more than one or two.

Stories of King Mswati's father speculated that he had had more than 200 wives. Even if Mswati had ten or so, that was a considerable difference from the example of his late father.

I certainly had no problem with respecting "tradition and culture" unless it interfered with practices and reform that would help Swaziland advance while still giving culture and tradition its due. Examples of good reforms, in my mind, meant a variety of things— better anti-HIV/AIDS practices, more representative governance, more modern business and investment policies, more jobs, better economic opportunity for women, among many others.

However, there were many vocal "protectors of the culture" out there who were quick to condemn reform as being "anti-Swazi culture", and in my view sometimes at the expense of needed progress.

On one of my visits to meet with the King, I decided to try to have a frank discussion with him about the overriding problem of HIV in Swaziland and what could be done by the country's leadership, meaning the King himself, to try to set a good example that could be seen by the population and help change behavior. For example, fighting the resistance to "knowing one's status" by getting tested, to more fidelity to one's partner, to awareness of the "AIDS orphans" crisis, to treatment options and so on.

"Your Majesty, do you mind if I speak frankly to you?" I asked. "No," he answered, "from you I am used to it," and he said it in a nice way so I continued.

"Your Majesty, if the only thing that outsiders know about Swaziland is that you have sixteen wives and buy them a BMW and a villa and that you have the highest rate of HIV/AIDS in the world, I submit, with all due respect, that you have a problem".

The King replied, "No, Ambassador, you are mistaken. I only have fourteen wives; two of the sixteen are fiancées...."

I don't remember the rest of the conversation but I remember being stunned by the response.

I had recently been out with the head of WFP observing the distribution of food to local communities and households—some headed by children as AIDS had killed their parents—and some of these in close proximity to the King's opulent palace.

I really wanted to convince the King and his principals to do more about the crisis happening right under their noses. I had tried to use humor, Southern humor, stories from the Bible and every other sort of tactic I could think of, but the response about the number of wives and fiancées had smacked me back into reality.

There were many good people in Swaziland doing their utmost to fight HIV by promoting status testing, distributing condoms, providing ARVs, fighting against mother-to-child transmission, promoting male circumcision, and providing treatment, but one thing was clear and it was unfortunate: I knew that looking to the Palace for leadership was mostly a waste of time.

There were about 200 Americans living in Swaziland, most doing great work—HIV/AIDS workers, missionaries—and most of those worked with hospitals and orphans—a writer or two, nuns, a couple of UN employees, Peace Corps volunteers and even a few US Bahai farmers for good measure.

I tried to visit as many as I could over the course of my stay in Swaziland. The nuns lived in the south where, during the hot months, the black mamba snakes were everywhere, causing the nuns to have aggressive little dogs to hunt them and scare them away.

The Peace Corps numbered some eighty or so volunteers making it one of the more robust programs in Africa. I visited some of the volunteers in the villages and saw some good work underway from what we called the "super volunteers". I liked the Peace Corps for the small-scale work they did but also due to the fact that it made the volunteers Africa and internationally-minded for life, and that was a good thing.

We were way off the map for CODELs—I assumed they were still going to Costa Rica—but got a few businessmen and State Department-sponsored musicians and speakers as well.

Mbabane actually had a sister-city in the US that turned out to be Fort Worth, Texas, our second favorite city in Texas. One day, we found out that some ninety-five Fort Worthians were coming to Mbabane, led by the Mayor, members of the City Council, a few senior police officers and other local dignitaries.

Joy and I invited them all over to the residence one evening, hanging the Texas flag on the wall and having a great time. The delegation had brought—God bless them—cowboy hats and boots for the Mbabane city council. For the next evening, we had found an actual country-western band in Swaziland and rented a restaurant as a dance hall. Everyone was decked out appropriately in cowboy hats and boots. I felt totally at home and happy.

The Swazis kept referring to the Fort Worth Mayor as "Your Worship", which sent the Texas delegation into hoots of laughter. We all stood for the playing of both countries' national anthems, but when it was time to play the "Star Spangled Banner" what came out was "God Save the Queen". Oops!

We were all shocked at first but dutifully stood and nobody said a word about it. The evening was a great success.

———

Before I left Africa, or before it was too late, I wanted to somehow meet with Nelson Mandela, a true savior of peace in South Africa and a longtime hero for his selfless struggle against apartheid and for majority rule. My predecessor as Ambassador had managed to meet Mandela, and I kept trying to figure a way to pull it off too, but alas I was busy where I was and Mandela was in Johannesburg and increasing hard to see given health and other age related issues.

Perhaps the next best thing, however, was to meet F.W. de Klerk who, as the last apartheid President of South Africa, had finally freed Mandela from his Robbens Island prison and permitted free and fair elections to proceed in 1994, thus ensuring majority rule.

Mandela's heart was set on reconciliation, not revenge, and it was remarkable to see South Africa go from being the site of an emerging racial war to a new day of possibility and peace, or at least something like it. Though not a perfect process by any means, it was better than the alternative. De Klerk had helped enable both Mandela and a new South Africa.

I had come to know a wealthy white Swazi entrepreneur by the name of Natie Kirsch, who now lived in the UK and in South Africa. Natie was in fact one of the richest men in Africa and was doing a lot, mostly behind the scenes, to contribute to economic opportunity and development in Swaziland and in South Africa.

Natie wanted to meet with Ambassadors to Swaziland from various key countries to get advice for an upcoming meeting with King Mswati. The idea was that he and De Klerk would try to prevail on the King to adopt better, more progressive and sensitive policies.

Only a handful of countries had full diplomatic embassies in Swaziland (even the Brits had recently downgraded their mission). But there was the US, neighboring South Africa, of course, and the Republic of China and a few more, the Ambassadors from other countries to Swaziland working mostly out of Pretoria or Maputo.

Swaziland was then one of the very few African countries that continued to recognize Taipei instead of Beijing. As of this writing, it is the only one still hanging on to Swaziland while Beijing brings in Chinese projects, Chinese workers and a monstrous debt burden for infrastructure projects that it has foisted on the rest of the continent.

The South African Ambassador to Swaziland was a former ANC fighter who told us and De Klerk that he was headed to the bush with a weapon in his hand to fight against apartheid when then President De Klerk released Mandela from prison and threw the doors open for free elections.

The two men embraced in a touching scene. With enthusiasm, De Klerk pronounced him "my fellow South African" in his booming voice. I felt I had just seen a little bit of history made and marveled at the sight of an embrace that even more likely could have once been, save for Mandela's and De Klerk's courage, a scene of violence rather than reconciliation.

The topography of Swaziland was diverse and I considered much of it flat out beautiful. Small mountains, grasslands, a few lush forests and, wonder of wonders, golf courses scattered around the country that invited many South African players—a stark difference juxtaposed to the much more marginal reality of most Swazis' lives.

Swaziland also had a series of game parks, and on the rare occasions when we had US visitors, that is where we would head first, though I took a few first to see the main HIV/AIDS hospital.

There was no hiding the fact that we were living in a country where right off the nice highways, regular Swazis struggled to live, feed their families, cope with the devastating effects of HIV/AIDS and just survive. With the loss of so many people due to HIV/AIDS complications and the proliferation of "AIDs orphans", there were far too many children being raised by children.

Swaziland was a monarchy and the King ruled as the last head of state monarch left in Africa. There was a Parliament too, but it was more or less a rubber stamp for the King. There were occasional protests for greater democracy by a few well-known groups and leaders, but sadly there didn't seem to be much meaningful dialogue between the reformers and the old guard, and I wondered just how long that tense relationship would last. Political parties were illegal in Swaziland, and had been for several decades.

Swaziland had a long way to go to become "a more representative government" which is a nice way of saying that regular Swazis had little to no role in affairs of government or state, civil society was weak, and existing institutions like the Parliament were equally weak. Despite all this, many in Swaziland seemed perfectly content to allow it stay that way.

I began to tire of the refrain repeated every day in the press or on the radio that almost any type of meaningful reform was antithetical to "Swazi tradition and culture."

My wife had gone home after a year to care for our son, so I was left "sans family" to finish my Ambassador term solo. There was plenty of valuable and interesting work left to do: an attempt to help reform and modernize Swaziland's investment promotion office, the design and kick-off of the rural enterprise project we undertook with the $10 million the State Department had told me about as I'd departed for post (which we leveraged financially into far more than the first mere $10 million), as well as work on implementing AGOA, the African Growth and Development Act.

Through AGOA we could identify locally produced products, mostly textiles, that could be exported to the US duty free, and we calculated we had already helped create some 30,000 jobs just in the Swazi textile industry alone through AGOA. Actually, after I departed Swaziland, the country was declared ineligible for that AGOA program for various reasons, but it was going full force while I was there and we took full advantage of it in trying to promote economic growth and employment.

More than anything, we had much more work to do on our HIV/AIDS program consolidation: prevention of mother-to-child transmission, knowing one's status, helping the Swazi government's internal management of its programs, all in coordination with CDC, the USG's seminal PEPFAR program, USAID's regional office in Pretoria, the World Health Organization, the Global Fund and especially the Swazis' own HIV/AIDS relief organization.

There was a long way to go on HIV/AIDS but the donors felt that we were putting together a program that would eventually result in a lower HIV/AIDS prevalence rate and save many lives.

I departed Swaziland for good with mixed feelings—frustration on one hand, but with a sense of accomplishment and gratitude for the good people with whom I had the good fortune to work on the other. Once my little passenger plane took off, I noted mentally that I was no longer Ambassador Lewis Lucke, and perhaps it was in that moment that I truly realized my good fortune at having served in such a position.

Haiti Earthquake

In January 2010, the Haiti earthquake happened. Some 200,000 Haitians were killed outright. I knew this was a disaster of Biblical proportions.

I had been in Haiti two months previously and had actually been encouraged by what I had seen—roads repaired, new businesses opening and a sense of optimism which was unlike my previous Haiti experiences.

That optimism was gone in an instant on the afternoon of January 26 when the ground shook, the epicenter almost dead center in Port au Prince where poorly constructed buildings collapsed or slid down hillsides.

I looked in horror at the devastation being shown on TV—this place I knew so well—and wondered what, if anything, I could do to help.

The former head of my USAID private sector office in Jordan, through a series of crazy events, had become the Acting Administrator of USAID. So, my friend Alonzo knew me and knew of my background in Haiti, that I spoke French, that I had the Ambassador title, and so forth. He called and asked me to come to Washington the next day to discuss the US earthquake response.

Long story short: I met the new Administrator of USAID, who had been named to his position just three days before the earthquake. I met the new Administrator and his people, conferred with my friend Alonzo and then asked, "What's next?"

Raj, the new Administrator, answered by saying that we had a flight out of Dulles in three hours to Port au Prince, and they needed me to be on it. My reply: "Okay, but what's my job?" A period of silence followed, which I had some trouble understanding but finally Raj answered the question: "You're in charge."

"In charge of what?" I asked.

"The whole thing," said Raj.

I came to understand that the Haiti earthquake response was to be a WOG ("Whole of Government") affair where various USG elements, along with a considerable military response, would be headed by USAID. That made sense in that USAID's Office of Foreign Disaster Assistance (OFDA) was, in essence, the "overseas FEMA" as mandated by law. With the US military bringing to bear its many assets, I knew that USAID's ability to lead, respond and coordinate effectively would be tested.

"Civ/mil collaboration", as it was called, was admittedly an imperfect art. It had not been done particularly well during the Iraq conflict, and there were more than a few lessons learned, as well as doctrine changes that would require more effective "civ/mil coordination". In Iraq, some military personnel hadn't a clue what USAID was or how we worked. As a result of that experience, more than a few of our USAID/OFDA people objected to working closely with the US military.

That was unacceptable, and much had evolved since then and, in such a case as a natural disaster, as was the Haiti earthquake, and the need to respond coherently and effectively, civilian/military cooperation was paramount.

The last thing Raj said to me as I headed out the door for Dulles: "The future of the Agency depends on how well we do."

No pressure there.

Next thing I knew, I was flying into Port au Prince as the head of the USAID's—actually the USG's—emergency response to the earthquake. Except there was an initial problem: the Port au Prince airport was so congested with incoming relief flights that we were waived off just a few meters above the tarmac—to where, I had no idea where.

It turned out we headed for the Turks and Caicos Islands some 90 miles north of Haiti's coast. Upon landing, the crew informed us that they had timed out and could not fly back to Haiti.

My first assignment in my new job was to meet Secretary of State Hillary Clinton later that same day as she disembarked at Port of Prince. The meeting was scheduled to take place in just a few hours, and I was stuck in the TCIs with no transportation.

I called a friend of mine in the White House—one of the few holdovers from the Bush Administration—and explained the problem. Richard was amazing. He said, "I will figure it out and get back to you." He called me back about five minutes later and said, "Walk out onto the tarmac and look to your left. You'll see a building on your left. That is a US Coast Guard station. They will fly you in by helicopter right now."

So I trotted to the Coast Guard hanger, boarded the helicopter and landed some forty-five minutes later at the Port-au-Prince airport. It was just two days after the earthquake and military and civilian aircraft were landing constantly with equipment and supplies. It would have been utter chaos except for the fact that the US Air Force was controlling the airport.

So I met Mrs. Clinton at the bottom of her plane's stairs as planned and then proceeded to meet with the Haitian President and Prime Minister. She had been briefed and knew my name. I also met my US military counterpart, who was the deputy commander of SOUTH-COM, General Ken Keen, a three-star.

I already knew Haitian President Préval because he had been president during my tenure as USAID/Haiti Mission Director, and though we in USAID weren't supposed to deal with governments, I'd met him several times when I was Charge' d'Affaires.

As an aside, I succeeded in making Mrs. Clinton angry at me. President Préval recognized me from before and spoke to me in French, and I answered him in French. Apparently, Mrs. Clinton did not appreciate the fact that I was speaking French.

If looks could have killed, I would be deader than dead, eviscerated, shredded, mangled, chewed up and spit out.

It seemed to me that when a chief of state greets you in his own language knowing full well that you speak that language, it would be polite and appropriate to briefly respond in that language. Or so it would seem. However, I could tell that the Secretary was not "d'accord", as it would be said in French...

Anyway, I rolled up my sleeves and went to work. The next thing I remember, it was three months later. It was amazing to be part of it, and I have to give much credit to our men and women in uniform, our own employees, a hundred NGOs, the international community and the UN.

Although I had some top USAID people and a great OFDA team, General Keen, my military counterpart, had as many as 30 full colonels plus 21,000 troops on land or at sea. I told General Keen that it was a little strange that the USAID guy was supposedly in charge of such an operation when it was DOD with all the assets, but we just accepted it and worked together to get the job done.

Those early days of the Haiti response we called the "hair on fire" days. It was absolute pandemonium. There were bodies in the streets. Rubble was everywhere. I could never have imagined such a disaster.

Many of the top people in the UN in Haiti had been killed and many of the survivors seemed to be in shock. The US military had to fill gaps, but at the same time we had to operate as part of an international operation and give respect and deference to the Haitians. We had a large and robust USAID DART team—Disaster Assistance Response Team—very capably led, as our point of the spear.

We took stock of experts in logistics, health, shelter, water/sanitation and so forth, trying to cover the landscape of needs. We also had to work with a Haitian government that was not particularly well functioning even in the best of times but had lost key people in the earthquake too.

We had to deal also with a UN organization that had been decimated by the earthquake and it was the UN that was supposed to lead when a disaster of this nature happens. We, therefore, had to be sensitive to all the damaged and injured partners and try to fill in the gaps where we could with our experts, either military or civilian. It was complete and utter chaos to start with, but every day it got a little better. We were flooded with requests every day—send a helicopter to this orphanage, take water to this place; something terrible has happened here, get security for another place, and so forth. We were also flooded with thousands of volunteers wanting to help.

The worst thing I had to deal with was a completely uncooperative USAID Mission Director, who had arrived in-country just as the earthquake struck. For some reason she assumed I was either up to no good or was trying to take her job (I had had her job ten years prior). She was becoming a detriment to our work, and our bosses back in Washington refused to deal with the issue. I later concluded that she was probably suffering from PTSD and probably would not have acted the way she did under different circumstances.

We had so many folks arrive who were ill prepared—no cell phone, no place to stay, no defined place to work, but they were there. I think hundreds were sleeping on the Embassy lawn at the start. God bless them, you can't blame people like that for trying to help, but it was hard to deal with them while we tried to manage a complex operation.

Nevertheless, we succeeded in getting many of them employed with NGOs or other groups. We had no cell phone coverage at the start but that was fixed fairly quickly. Literally, there were dead bodies to be buried and mountains of rubble that would take years to remove.

The Embassy building—itself a new structure which had been built to earthquake standards had sustained little damage—had to operate under never-intended circumstances. People were sleeping on the floors, and each workspace was overcrowded, so OFDA set up a tent at the rear of the Embassy compound.

General Keen and I met daily with the US Ambassador and kept him briefed. He was helpful to an extent, but it was clear that what he really wanted was for all us earthquake responders to go away as soon as possible and let him have his Embassy back. The Ambassador's residence had to be architecturally assessed before he could move back in, so he slept in his office on a cot.

The Montana Hotel, where I had stayed on several occasions, was the center of rescue groups from many countries, all trying to pull survivors out of the rubble. A group of US college students had been staying there and soon their story was receiving global attention.

Our best asset, of course, was the US military with all their equipment, helicopters and various skill sets. I was quickly becoming a big fan of helicopters and did a lot of country-wide coverage thanks to them and to General Keen. I was incredibly grateful every day for the US military and their amazing capabilities.

Roads were clogged with debris and then with traffic, so it was hard and time consuming to rely on vehicles. If I could go by helicopter, I did. General Keen always had a helicopter at his disposal, so we made a lot of joint trips.

It was important to point out that our phase of the earthquake response was only for emergency rescue and immediate recovery and not reconstruction. That would come later, and for many reasons, I wanted no part of the official reconstruction effort that would far outlast our shorter rescue and recovery phase.

After dealing with the bodies, we had to assess the water, food and medical situation, and that, for us, was the task of the DART. It became clear that there wasn't a water or food shortage, but rather a distribution issue. We had to deal with port problems and basically soon brought in an artificial port in the form of a large barge from a US company. That helped with the delivery of food, medical assistance and water in the early days. We had to manage distribution, deal with logistical logjams and solve a thousand other problems happening all around us.

As previously mentioned, we were very concerned with the Montana Hotel where a lot of foreigners had been staying, including the US college students, diplomats, and a few military officers. We knew this was going to be a tragedy.

We deployed two US rescue teams on contract with OFDA, one of them from Arlington, Virginia, and one from Los Angeles. There were teams from the US, Chile, France and even Iceland working at the Montana site. Our DART did a good job, doing what they do best, a lot of it having to do with assessments to identify problems and issues.

The Chileans were running the Montana site as they were the first to arrive at the scene. They were especially motivated as the wife of one Chilean official had been at the Montana's fitness center when the earth quake hit and they controlled the site until her body was found in the rubble. Rescue dogs squeezed in and out of the debris, in the early days finding live survivors and later finding only bodies.

One of the owners of the Montana, whom I had known when I was working in Haiti previously, was found after four days trapped in the rubble, battered but alive. She eventually recovered. Another was found alive in the area of what had been the hotel bar and was able to survive by drinking what she could find in the immediate area. Many others were not so fortunate. The kind Haitian bartender who had taught me how to make rum sours only a few weeks before was among the dead.

We worked through what the UN calls, and what we all called, the cluster system, which meant groups to assess and address areas such as housing, water, health, sanitation, etc. The UN slowly replaced their missing personnel who had been killed, and the cluster system got on its feet. I knew some of the UN people—two of the top UN representatives had been friends of mine in other countries.

A key official of the World Food Program (WFP) arrived from the Rome headquarters and was very effective in unblocking food assistance that had been initially held up. The lead UN guy was an American named Tony whom I had also known from my post-Swaziland days in Rome where we'd both worked for a while with the

WFP. Tony was essential in getting the UN back up and operating and helping to solve so many problems. We worked well together.

The other factor that proved to be propitious was that General Keen had gone to staff college with the head of the UN military peacekeeping team called MINUSTAH (United Nations Stabilization Mission in Haiti—French initials). He was a Brazilian general. The fact that General Keen and the Brazilian general already knew each other was another stroke of luck and made interaction easier.

One of the main challenges we had to deal with had nothing to do with us or Haiti, but rather in dealing with Washington. This was early in the Obama Administration and their tendency was to try to overmanage or micromanage everything from Washington, which is impossible to do anyway and made our lives more complicated.

Our USAID group acquired more qualified people over time, but the pace was killing us: I had people literally dropping from exhaustion, and it happened frequently! People were working twenty hours a day under great pressure. After a while, they just fell apart. I would tell workers that this was a marathon, not a sprint, and to take care of themselves.

I found that I was not particularly good at taking my own advice and came close to falling apart myself. I literally had key staff passing out from exhaustion, including doctors. Working in those conditions was very hard, but people were very dedicated to the task at hand and the work got done. I was grateful for such a dedicated group that could accomplish so much under difficult circumstances.

I should probably mention that in the early days of the response, we were beset by hundreds of individual responders including a few celebrities from Hollywood: first John Travolta, Sean Penn, Patricia Arquette, and I'm sure many more I never knew about and wouldn't have known anyway.

Having been overseas for the greater part of three decades, I had missed much of US popular culture and was out of touch regarding celebrities. I guess I expected the celebs would fly in a planeload of stuff, have a news conference with lots of photographers, probably clog up the airport and then depart for good.

To my surprise, Sean Penn was not like that. He came to stay for the duration and brought an NGO team and funding with him. He started a relief camp on the old Petionville golf course and was soon providing effective assistance to hundreds of Haitians who had lost everything.

When he admitted to General Keen and me that he didn't really know what he was doing, we had him admitted to the UN cluster coordination effort. He would put on his JP/HRO (his NGO) baseball hat and his newly issued UN ID and attended the necessary meetings like everyone else.

I met and spoke with him on a few occasions, and even went to a dinner with him at one surviving outdoor Petionville restaurant. He was normal and congenial and, like Louis IV or maybe the Pope, carried no cash with him. He also didn't know anything about Haitian rum either, on which I tried to enlighten him.

Sean and I would never have agreed on anything political (he supported Hugo Chavez of Venezuela, for example), but he was serious about helping Haiti and he and his good people did so effectively and selflessly.

One of our first tasks was to create a work force of Haitians who could clear rubble with small tools in order to provide them an income and permit them to buy food and support their families while providing a much needed stimulus to the almost destroyed local economy. UNDP did the same thing. Our workers were provided yellow T-shirts with the UN providing blue ones. Without these programs, large numbers of Haitians willing and able to work would have remained idle and without income.

Tent camps of IDPs (internally displaced persons), had sprung up all over Port au Prince and the surrounding area. Whole neighborhoods had been destroyed, or buildings were so damaged that the former inhabitants were afraid to reoccupy them. Tent cities sprang up seemingly wherever the victims could find an open space.

It became clear that we had to begin to address the shelter issue in a more organized way. Scores of camps—some with many tents and some with few—were now sheltering much of the population. Soon the UN and the rest of the donor community was working hard to assure food and clean water to the camps and making plans to provide temporary but stable shelter to the thousands doing without. This issue would soon become critical as the rainy season was fast approaching.

Adequate shelter became one of the premier issues for relief, after providing food, water, and medicine. We knew that we had a huge problem in terms of shelter. So many Haitians suffered from inadequate housing in the best of times, but it became one of the most severe issues after the earthquake.

Addressing shelter was an international effort, not just USAID, so the international effort began to focus on shelter via the provision and distribution of thousands of tarps as opposed to tents. Tarps are a lot better than tents because tents tear, fly away and eventually rot. In the context of Haiti, a temporary shelter with a tarp could eventually, more or less, be transformed into a more stable and more durable shelter than a tent. We used to give the "think outside the tent" speech a lot in favor of tarps versus tents.

I had a conversation with President Clinton—a fairly regular presence in Haiti by then—about this at the airport. He told me he could bring in tens of thousands of tents from Bangladesh. I gave him the "tarp versus tent" speech and politely told him to please *not* send us any more tents.

Victims themselves of the quake, the UN and its cluster system finally became better equipped and staffed to deal with food, logistics, water and shelter and a host of other issues. The Haitian government was as helpful as they could be under the circumstances, and a few capable and key host-country staff came forward. We never lost sight of the fact that this was their country and they had to be the face of the recovery effort to whatever extent possible.

My own staff grew as we begged, borrowed and stole key staff members from others. A few former FEMA experts joined us, I 'stole' a debris removal expert, a former NYC fireman who was also with FEMA and had worked at Ground Zero after 9/11. Mike was a godsend, and I even taught him how to say in French, "I am the head of rubble removal" i.e. *"Je suis le chef du degas"*...

I also got the "amazing Richard" of Turks and Caicos fame from the White House to help us too. I was even eventually able to recruit some USAID veterans from other countries that I knew and trusted—my new Deputy was Chris from Iraq days, and my old guitar-playing colleague Peter from Bolivia plus a host of hard-working and dedicated newbies including a group of Creole-speaking Haitian Americans already with USAID.

As a sign that we were finally getting organized, we started to receive CODEL visitors every Monday. Many of these—but not all—were Obama-era Democrat Congressmen and Congresswomen: House Speaker Pelosi, Charlie Rangel, Sheila Jackson Lee of Houston (who used to phone me in Iraq sending me into panic mode), Maxine Waters, John Conyers and a whole host of others who needed briefings, logistical support and so forth. Bill Clinton came too, often on his own plane and usually with Cheryl Mills, Mrs. Clinton's Chief of Staff, in tow.

General Keen and I would normally brief the CODELs while on their plane, then load up the vehicles and take them around Port au Prince to assess the situation. One poignant scene happened when we dropped Congresswomen Pelosi, Waters and Lee at the ruined and mostly collapsed National Cathedral. They held hands in front of one of the few remaining parts of the formerly lovely Cathedral—a large stone cross. One of the male Congressmen on the plane following my briefing and in response to my request for questions, asked me, "What is USAID doing here in first place?"

Thanks, Congressman, for your kind vote of support.

Maxine Waters is the one who mystified me the most. She came to the Embassy for several days in a row apparently to observe us to see if we were working. She would sit in our modest-sized DART room on one side of the table, down-turned mouth and down-turned eyes, with not a single document in front of her, and just stare at us. This would go on for hours at a time. Several of her Congressional staff sat on the other side of the table and did the same thing.

This, we considered, was strange behavior (did she think we were just telling jokes, playing cards and eating bonbons?) and they were frankly in the way, but we were too busy to worry about it and we all knew we had no control over these people. So we just kept working.

I engaged Congressman Rangle in conversation at one point and told him we had met years ago in Costa Rica. He was still engaging, interested and agreeable.

I was called onto Bill Clinton's plane at the airport on two occasions to brief him—Cheryl Mills was there once—and his questions were informed and he was easy to talk to. I didn't bother to remind him that I had previously briefed him on Iraq in late 2003 when we were both in Qatar. He held an unlit and probably very expensive cigar in his left hand, which I noticed trembled slightly.

With the CODELs, once we were in our vehicles the briefings were supposed to continue and we were available to answer any questions they might have. This was the era when one of the constant refrains about the economy, foreign affairs and much else was "Bush's fault". Once when waiting for a Congressional straggler, I started talking to a Congressman from Fort Worth loud enough that others in the van could hear.

"You know that scientists have been evaluating the tectonic plates under Port au Prince that caused the earthquake? You know what its name is?" "No," the Texas Congressman replied. "It's Bush's Fault." A laugh followed from the Congressman.

Silence followed from all the others and I concluded that they either had no sense of humor or completely didn't get it. Okay, back to the briefing...

After the initial "hair on fire" days and a couple of weeks into the relief effort, it became apparent that there actually was no serious shortage of food or water in and around Port au Prince. The issue was distribution, so the WFP food NGOs and OFDA's food NGOs worked hard to assure something like an orderly distribution system in the capital area.

Haitian recipients would gather at the distribution points and pass through a ring of security, pick up a predetermined amount of food—normally rice—and then depart the area. This process became more orderly as time progressed but initially we heard stories of bandits robbing food recipients after they had left the area.

Often the security ring was provided by US soldiers who seemed to take their jobs seriously. I asked a few soldiers some questions when I was observing the effort: "Did you think you would be doing this kind of work when you joined the military?" An emphatic "No" was the inevitable reply. "How do like doing this kind of work now that you're doing it?" They invariably replied, "We love it. It's positive and makes us feel proud and useful."

After two months or so, the US military had started to draw down its deployment numbers and the hospital ship, the USS Hope, previously anchored off the coast of the capital, had left the area. The military assets were fewer in number because they were no longer needed. Distribution points for food were well established and did not have to be guarded. Everything was falling into place for a more controllable relief effort.

One of the cardinal rules of development and disaster response is *do no harm*, so we didn't want to continue food or water distribution at the expense of the private sector markets. Agriculture in Haiti had been very negatively affected by US policies under the Clinton Administration, and we didn't want to make it any worse. We did what we needed to do to assure food, water and medicine right after the earthquake, but there was no need to do it forever, or even past the immediate emergency phase, and in fact to do so would have been harmful.

Things were getting back to normal and the local economy was coming back to life, but so many people were still living in temporary shelters, and there was the huge task ahead of clearing away the rubble, a process that would take several years. Rubble was slowly moved to a landfill outside Port Au Prince.

Another priority for us after getting some 300,000 tarps distributed was to unclog all the canals in Port au Prince that had been filled with rubble and garbage. That was an urgent undertaking because if the canals were not cleared, there would have been floods in the city once the rainy season started. We accomplished the task with a corps of hard working and experienced NGOs who brought in heavy equipment and local workers.

We always had a pressing priority of the day, or a priority of the week, or a priority of the month. We identified each priority and tried to get them done as quickly as we could by using a "tasking" system to pass the request for action on to the military where they were the appropriate implementor.

One of the great advantages of working through OFDA, the Office of Foreign Disaster Assistance, was that the grant process was truncated and could quickly be carried out. Grants could be awarded to NGOs in a few minutes, as opposed to weeks, because the law provided them special authority to move the money quickly. OFDA would not have been effective otherwise.

Soon our two emergency rescue teams from Virginia and California that OFDA had kept on standby packed up and departed. They had done amazing and even heroic work, and I was at the airport to shake their hands and thank them in person as they filed onto their planes.

The CODELs continued however and we soon got word that we would receive Presidents Bush 43 and Clinton, planning to arrive in separate small jets at the same time. I met and greeted Bush 43 as we watched Clinton's jet land and park beside 43's. Except, true to form, Clinton was late and stayed in his plane for some reason while Bush 43 cooled his heels, though he soon found a number of military personnel on the tarmac to meet and greet and pose for photos.

Finally, after what had become a bit of an awkward situation, Clinton made his exit from his jet onto the tarmac, greeted Bush 43 and then the party with their small entourages made their way to our vehicles. Both presidents posed for photographers in front of the now destroyed Presidential Palace. They then proceeded to give short remarks to a crowd of officials and dignitaries and then headed in an animated crowd of Haitian IDPs, surrounded by their tents, tarps and detritus who struggled to see the presidents up close or answer a hurried question or two posed by the visitors.

I tried to surround myself with good people that I knew could do the job, and as it turned out I knew a lot of these people from Iraq. The person who ended up replacing me as US Response Coordinator was my former deputy from Iraq, Chris. It was still impossible for us in USAID to keep up with General Keen's ability to muster thousands of troops and a gaggle of full Colonels to fill out his staff. We did the best we could, but it was clear that our personnel system was not equipped to respond quickly to emergencies like the Haiti earthquake.

We had a USAID/Military senior staff meeting early every morning and we contributed what we could. It seemed to me that a good number of General Keen's officers must have spent many hours a day preparing powerpoint slides about all aspects of the relief effort as their presentation occupied much of every meeting. The slides seemed endless, and as I had trouble reading the small print, I wondered exactly who had decided that power point slides were all that essential. I was just glad that it wasn't me who had to prepare those slides, but the colonels didn't complain.

My staff spent an equal amount of time in meetings with Haitian officials and especially with the multiple UN agencies that had been slowly reconstituted and re-staffed and dealt with the entire gamut of issues—all urgent—such as food, the start of debris removal. organizing and caring for tent camps that had sprung up everywhere, with unblocking the port—especially medical supplies—assuring water delivery and, increasingly important, the delivery and distribution of thousands of tarps that would provide better protection for people than the thousands of tents that had been the first line of defense but would have tended to rot, blow away and impede the better tarp solution had we not brought them in as quickly as possible.

There was no reasoning with hurricane season, as Jimmy Buffet may have once eloquently stated, so getting tarps distributed was essential.

Speaking of Jimmy Buffet, an announcement was made at the Embassy one fine mid-day that one Mr. Buffet was playing a mini-concert in the back of the Embassy and all were invited. I thought it was a joke but when I checked it out between meetings, there he was. He enlisted a few Coast Guard ladies (corpsmen, corpswomen?) as back-up singers and winged it through a couple of songs.

The work day was always long, and nine of us who were crowded into a largely intact apartment across the street from the Embassy made the best of it. For a while I tried to take Ambien in order to sleep quickly, so after four or so hours of sleep I could proceed on to the next long and stress-filled day.

Note to self: taking Ambien and thinking you can operate normally after a few hours' sleep is not recommended and can render you immobile. I learned that the hard way when I started our normal morning staff huddle, my mouth opened and absolutely nothing came out. Chris jumped in to run the huddle, and surely thought that I was losing it. No more Ambien, no matter what.

Finally, after two months or more, things were getting back to some sense of normalcy. Food and water were available again through normal systems and medical services were again being slowly provided by local doctors and hospitals. There was an initial hue and cry about the departure of the hospital ship *USS Hope*, but it was soon determined that the cost of its continued presence was not worth the symbolic value of having it remain in port.

Bit by bit, we transformed from an emergency operation to one of recovery, and eventually reconstruction. Cell phones were widely available and functional again, rubble removal was beginning but with what would be years of work ahead, some IDP camps were decreasing in number, medicine was available locally, and port repair was underway. The artificial port we'd had towed in from Florida at great expense went home. The military was drawing down and re-deploying. The helicopter carrier USS Bataan that had been stationed off the coast of Port au Prince and had provided essential rescue and medevac services also left its offshore station and re-deployed.

Much to the relief of the Ambassador, the Embassy was getting back to normal, people were no longer sleeping on the floors, and badges were again being inspected by our Marine security detachment. The DART emergency response and rescue teams closed shop, packed up and went home. They had done an amazing job. Many of the other participants like NGOs, the UN and the entire international community had pitched in and had provided an effective, however imperfect, response.

Knowing Haiti's history and current situation well, my personal hope was that though since so much in Haiti had been destroyed, that what was to be built would be better than it was before. That said, Haiti has a long history of dashed hopes, institutionalized corruption, predatory politics, ineffective governance and intractable poverty to overcome. Through it all, my admiration and love for these people was reconfirmed by my Haiti earthquake experience.

There were many lessons learned on civ/mil collaboration from prior natural or man-made disasters—the Pakistan earthquake response, Iraq and so forth—and many subsequent civilian and military seminars were held to spread the news of how we did what we did and how others who might be in similar situations could prepare.

General Keen and I participated in such events at the National War College, and another at the Pacific Command (PACOM), where top military and diplomatic attendees came from all over Asia to listen.

While there will always be those "hair on fire" days for disaster responses, it is also true that proper planning prevents poor performance, and understanding those "lessons learned" from prior disasters would be key to that planning. The US part of the Haiti earthquake response, however imperfect, is now seen as an example of effective civilian/military collaboration that saved many lives, responded to immediate needs and gave Haiti a chance to rebuild.

Epilogue

I FIRST WENT OVERSEAS with the USAID Foreign Service in 1978 to Bamako, Mali. My other countries followed and a few of my experiences—by no means all or even most—are recounted in this book. After retirement from the State Department in 2006, I even put myself on the bench for short-term recall assignments on missions to Brazil, the Democratic Republic of the Congo, Jordan, Mauritania, Saudi Arabia (working on Yemen), Djibouti (twice) and finally to East Timor.

Though I was working mostly in the private sector by then with my own companies, I still loved being involved in the work overseas and made the time for some of the offered overseas assignments. The Foreign Service, then and now, needs smart, multilingual, culturally adaptable, creative, hardworking and competent people to do it. This has not changed over the years and will not in the future. It was, as usual, interesting and valuable work.

Hopefully I made a positive contribution to US and host-country strategies and ambitions. Some of the work helped make host country institutions better. Some of it made a big difference in the lives of mostly poor people, including so many women, and through both economic development and disaster response programs lives were improved and sometimes saved.

One more benefit: The work was fun and it was satisfying. I never had a boring day. When I take time to reflect on it, my conclusion is, "What a blessing it all was!"

As a senior USAID manager, I always tried to run our overseas mission as much like a business as one could—goal oriented, results driven, focused and resolute—so I felt fully comfortable with my post-Foreign Service private sector activities and goals. As far as USAID programs went, my mantra was "be a mile deep not a mile wide"; i.e. focus and do a few things extremely well and ignore some

164

of the peripheral stuff. If you try to do everything you think you should do, you risk failure and dilute your impact. This was important as results matter and we were always dealing with, literally, other peoples' money.

Some things in my view have changed for the worse: there is less "delegation of authority" to the field than previously; we have become more slavish to reporting and monitoring/evaluation/indicators as ends in themselves rather than helpful tools. As far as USAID goes, we transformed to spending most of our time monitoring the work of others—contract partners, NGOs, etc—rather than doing most of it ourselves.

Headquarters now controls and requires too many approvals than needed, and though it is better at this writing than in recent years, the "thousand mile long screwdriver" is still there.

From a family perspective, I was lucky in that I ended up with the same wife I started with (and who excelled in her own overseas work) and had three, now fully-grown and successful children, all with those essential elements—a sense of responsibility and a sense of humor. Foreign Service kids seem to mature a little faster than their domestic peers and are comfortable with adults, foreign cultures and weird situations.

Colleagues told me that some Foreign Service kids grew up to become ill-adapted to life in the US and strove to go abroad again as soon as possible. Others were perfectly happy to go home, get an education and stay home. Travel, yes; but live, not necessarily. The latter description fits all three of our kids.

I recall my kids reaching the "age of reason" and turning to their mother and me and saying, "You never told us living in the US (actually they said 'Texas') was so nice."

They figured that out for themselves, and while they loved their overseas friends and experiences, they were not wholly defined by them. In fact, with families and issues of their own, they rarely, if ever, initiate talking about it.

I appreciate the help of many in putting this book together—first to my wife Joy for initial proofreading, as well as my friends and former colleagues, Jeff Goodson, Rafael Jabba and Alex Newton, who offered valuable insights and recommendations at the right time. Rafael was particularly helpful in recalling and recounting key parts of the Iraq chapter.

Special thanks too to my editors at Open Books, particularly the ever patient and steady David Ross who continued to make valued suggestions throughout the process and channeled my sometimes too-wicked sense of humor into better prose.

I also should acknowledge three special Foreign Service colleagues I directly served with who died along the way, two in active service and one following retirement. Ferebee Lewis, my kind and valued administrative assistant in Tunisia, died in Cairo on Christmas day 1993 after her apartment was sprayed with a pesticide that was not permitted for such use in the US. The irrepressible Margaret Alexander, Deputy Mission Director in Nepal and my Legal Advisor in Haiti, died in a helicopter crash in 2006 in the Himalayas.

Dr. Gerald Cashion, a main subject of my first book about Mali, *Waiting for Rain: Life & Development in Mali, West Africa*, passed in 2019 after a long health struggle. Gerry was my dear friend, instructor on all things Mali, inspiration on economic development, my sailing buddy, the best Irish anthropologist imaginable, and possessing an infinite well of kindness, knowledge and humor.

One last obligatory note: The opinions offered in this book are mine and mine alone and do not represent the views or policy of the US Agency for International Development (USAID) or the US Department of State.

Annex 1

Washington Demands and Disaster Assistance: USAID and the 2010 Haiti Earthquake

From *The Association of Diplomatic Studies & Training: Interview by Sabrina Rostkowski*

LEWIS LUCKE WAS CALLED out of retirement in 2010 to coordinate USAID's response to the disastrous 7.0 magnitude Haitian earthquake, which killed an estimated 100,000 people and dealt a devastating blow to a country still reeling from political instability and the aftermath of a military coup. Lucke found bodies in the street and mountains of rubble, a "magnificent" U.S. military response and a persistent challenge in meeting Washington's incessant demands for information. "At one point, it seemed that my bosses in Washington felt my main job was to prepare powerpoint presentations so they could show them to Obama," Lucke recalled. "I told them if that was what they thought was my job, that I would quit right now and be gone." Ex-President Clinton also visited Haiti during Lucke's three-month assignment there. At an airport meeting, Clinton "told me he could bring in thousands of tents from Bangladesh, I think it was," Lucke said. "I gave him the 'tarp vs tent' speech and politely told him to please NOT bring us any more tents."

Lucke remained in Haiti for three backbreaking months, joining forces with the UN, a Disaster Assistance Response Team (DART) from USAID, a multitude of NGOs, and thousands of volunteers. He found Haiti's capital, Port-au-Prince, almost completely destroyed. "The Presidential palace was a beautiful building," he recalled, "but most of it was now collapsed and had to be bulldozed away as rubble." Another major blow was the destruction of the headquarters of the United Nations Stabilization Mission in Haiti, killing the Mission's chief and 95 other UN personnel. This severely handicapped the UN's capacity for emergency response.

Lucke had previously served as USAID Mission Director in Haiti, and was an obvious choice to coordinate the agency's response to the earthquake. When the call came to return to Haiti, Lucke was preparing to return after an illustrious career that had taken him to Mali, Senegal, Costa Rica, Tunisia, Bolivia, Jordan, Haiti, Iraq after the Second Gulf War, and an Ambassadorship in Swaziland.

Annex 2

USAID Accomplishments in Iraq: One Year, April 2003-March 2004

Restoring Essential Infrastructure:

Electricity: with other partners like the Ministry of Electricity and the US Army Corps of Engineers, we worked to restore the capacity of Iraq's power systems which was degraded from years of neglect, mismanagement and looting.

Progress as of March 2004: Generation of 4,518 MW of electricity, surpassing the pre-war level of 4,108 MW; generation reached 98,917 MW hours in mid-February, the highest since reconstruction began; independent power sources installed at Baghdad International Airport and Umm Qasr seaport; repairs of thermal units, turbines and the transmission network to produce 2,152 MW of additional capacity; maintenance and rehabilitation of gas turbine and diesel units for another 1020 MW of capacity. Rehabilitating two units of the Dora power plant, rehabilitation of five units at the Bayji plant; reconstructing 220 kilometers of 400—kv transmission lines and installing new generation capacity at power plants at Kirkuk and S. Baghdad.

Airports: Repairing damaged airport facilities, rehabilitating airport terminals; facilitating humanitarian and commercial flights; and preparation of airport operations to handover to Iraqi control.

Progress as of March 2004: Terminals and admin offices repaired; 5000-plus military and NGO flights arrived and departed since July 2003; twenty commercial flights a day; x-ray machines installed; new communications systems and generators installed; airport fire station and customs hall rehabilitated; large array of airport repairs at Basrah Airport finished.

Bridges and Railroads: Rehabilitating and repairing damaged transportation systems, especially economically critical networks

Progress as of March 2004: Bridges: Demolished irreparable sections of three bridges and started reconstruction; four lane bridge on Highway 10 between Jordan and Baghdad repaired and reopened to traffic; other bridges key to commerce and agriculture repaired and reopened; Tigris river bridge at Al Kut repaired, improving traffic for about 50,000 travelers a day. Railroads: track repairs at Um Qasr port and 56 km of track near Basrah to facilitate delivery of cargo shipments; completed ordinance disposal at fifty-three rail project sites.

Umm Qasr Seaport: Managing port administration; coordinating transport from seaport; improved cargo-handling services such as storage and warehousing; renovating key offloading equipment.

Progress as of March 2004: Port reopened to commercial traffic, offloading of fifty cargo ships a month; port dredged to depth of 12.5 meters removing cargo offloading limitations; Iraqi dredger repaired; grains receiving facilities repaired; port tariffs instituted; generators installed; security fencing completed, admin, passenger and customs halls renovated; five hundred Iraqi staff hired.

Telecommunications: Restoring 240,000 telephone lines in Baghdad; repairing the fiber optics network in key regions.

As of March 2004: Al-Mamoun Telecommunication center repaired and handed over to Ministry of Communications; satellite gateway integrated with telephone and postal switches; tools and equipment procured to enable Iraqis to pursue further repairs; twenty cities restored to fiber optic network; switches installed for 240,000 landlines and new switches and distribution frames installed; largest exchange, Al-Mamoun, reopened; training of Iraqi engineers and operators undertaken.

Water & Sanitation: Rehabilitation and repairing of essential water infrastructure to provide potable water and sanitation to communities and improve irrigation

As of March 2004: Rehabilitation of sewage and water treatment plants effecting millions of Iraqis; repair of water conveyance systems throughout central and southern Iraq; repairing hundreds of breaks in the water distribution system significantly increasing water flow; repairs and increasing capacity by forty-five percent of Baghdad's water plant affecting overpopulated eastern sections of Baghdad; installation of backup generators at forty-one Baghdad water and pumping facilities; rehabilitation of Baghdad's sewage treatment plants; rehabilitation of seventy Baghdad non-functioning water pumping stations; Sweet Water Canal cleaned and reservoir cleanup began; generator at Karkh water treatment plant—Baghdad main water treatment facility—rehabilitated.

Health & Education: Supporting the Iraqi Ministry of Health, delivering essential health services, funding vaccines and high protein biscuits for pregnant and lactating women and malnourished children, establishing a rapid referral and response system for the most serious cases, providing basic primary health care equipment and supplies, training and upgrading health staff education.

As of March 2004: Procured more than 30 million doses of vaccines since July 2003 with support from the Ministry of Health and UNICEF; vaccinated 3 million children under the age of five through the Expanded Immunization Program since June 2003. USAID provided vaccines for 4.2 million children under five and 700,000 pregnant women; immunization catch-up immunization campaign with UNICEF and the Ministry of Health with 4,000 health workers and 124 supervisors; $1.8 million in small grants awarded to support Iraqi NGO healthcare efforts throughout Iraq; developed a hospital and clinic facility database for the Ministry of Health; renovated fifty-two primary health care clinics and re-equipping over 600 to provide essential primary healthcare services; trained 340 master trainers in eighteen governorates who trained 2,000-plus primary healthcare providers to treat and prevent acute respiratory infections and diarrheal diseases; distributed high-protein supplementary food rations to more than 240,000 pregnant and nursing mothers and malnourished children; surveyed eighteen national and regional public health laboratories for equipment needs; rehabilitated the National Polio Laboratory; one-thousand-plus health workers and volunteers trained to identify, treat and monitor the growth of acutely malnourished children; worked with the Iraqi MOH to develop a strategic plan to reduce child mortality and increase the level of preventative care available to the Iraqi people addressing public health, health care delivery, health information systems, pharmaceuticals, medical supplies and equipment, health care finance, education and training, human resources, legislation and regulation, and licensing and accreditation; distributed 1.4 million liters of clean water each day to people in the cities of Al Basrah, Al Muthanna', Kirkuk, and Mosul.

Education: Increasing enrollment and improving the quality of primary and secondary education, ensuring that classrooms have sufficient materials, facilitating community involvement, training teachers, implementing accelerated learning programs, and establishing partnerships between US and Iraqi colleges and universities.

As of March 2004: Provided technical assistance for the resumption of the Ministry of Education functions and salaries; funded 5.5 million examinations for transitional grades, which ensured the smooth continuation of school; surveyed secondary schools in all permissive areas of the country; awarded 627 grants worth more than $6 million to rehabilitate and equip schools; rehabilitated 2,360 schools countrywide in time for the first term of the 2003/04 school year; distributed nearly 1.5 million secondary school kits that included pens, pencils, paper, math equipment and other supplies; distributed 159,005 student desks, 26,437 teacher desks, 59,940 teacher chairs, 26,050 metal cabinets, 61,500 chalkboards, and 58,100 teacher kits: delivered 808,000 primary student kits and 81,000 primary teacher kits; with Iraqi Ministry of Education, reviewed forty-eight math and science textbooks for grades one through twelve; printed and distributed 8,759,260 textbooks throughout Iraq; trained 860 secondary school Master Trainers during September 2003 to January 2004 nationwide; trained 31,772 secondary school teachers and administration staff; conducted an accelerated learning program in Baghdad, Nasiriyah, Ad Diwaniyah, Karbala', and Erbil; helped the Fulbright Scholarship Program return to Iraq after a fourteen-year absence, awarding twenty-five scholarships for Iraqis to study in the United States; launched the Higher Education and Development Program, awarding five grants worth an estimated $20.7 million for US-Iraqi university partnerships with five US universities and seventeen Iraqi universities.

Economic Opportunity: Currency conversion and development of economic statistics, small businesses credits, commercial legislation, a national employment program, micro-finance programs, a bank-to-bank payment system, a computerized financial management information system, tax policy and administration, budget planning, insurance, telecommunications reform, and electricity reform.

As of March 2004: With the Ministry of Finance, introduced the new national currency, the Iraqi Dinar; a currency exchange was established; 6.36 trillion new Iraqi dinars arrived in country, and 4.62 trillion Iraqi dinars were in circulation; a daily currency auction for banks to exchange dinars and dollars began; seventy-seven thousand public works jobs were created through the National Employment Program: helped start implementation of a bank-to-bank payment system that allows eighty banks to send and receive payment instructions; with the Iraqi Treasury's work to reconcile and close the year-end 2003 financial statements of Iraq's two largest banks—the state-owned Rasheed and Rafidain; Assisted CPA in managing a $21-million microcredit program; supported CPA's Oil for Food (OFF) Program in planning, program management, logistics, database applications, and communications to support the CPA OFF Coordination Center in the north and south; updated commercial laws pertaining to private sector and foreign investment; assisted in the development of the new Company Law; Firm-Level Assistance Program is complete and program activity is commencing with 200 firms applying to the CPA Office of Private Sector Development to participate in the program, the activity will provide technical assistance to small-and medium-sized Iraqi companies in developing business plans.

Food Security: Providing oversight support for the countrywide public distribution system, which provides basic food and non-food commodities to an estimated 25 million Iraqis, participating in the design of a monetary assistance program to replace the commodity-based distribution system to support local production and free-market infrastructure, and promoting comprehensive agriculture reform to optimize private participation in production and wholesale markets.

As of March 2004: Worked with the UN World Food Program (WFP) and Coalition Forces to re-establish Iraq's public distribution system in less than thirty days thus avoiding an humanitarian food crisis and maintaining food security; contributed cash and food aid in the amount of $425 million to WFP's emergency operations immediately following the conflict, making the United States the foremost contributor to WFP emergency operations in Iraq; placed food specialists in Baghdad, Al Basrah, Al Hillah, and Erbil to support food operations immediately after the conflict. Provided ongoing support and technical assistance to WFP and local Iraqi authorities in the Ministry of Trade and the Kurdish Food Departments to ensure the smooth transition of public distribution system management tasks to the Iraqi government; helped negotiate a memorandum of understanding between the CPA, the Ministry of Trade, and the World Food Program that details WFP's areas of responsibility to include: capacity building and training, procurement of food commodities, the renegotiation of certain food contracts, shipment and overland transport of food commodities, and pipeline management; provided food aid expertise to CPA and Ministry of Trade in Baghdad and assisting with the CPA OFF Coordination Center as WFP and CPA and the Ministry continue to distribute food to all Iraqis.

Agriculture: Expanding agricultural productivity, restoring the capacity of agro-enterprises to produce, process, and market agricultural goods and services, nurturing access to rural financial services, and improving land and water resource management.

As of March 2004: USAID partner DAI implements the Agricultural Reconstruction and Development Program for Iraq (ARDI) to formulate a long-term vision for the sector, while designing activities for quick impact including: Winter Crop Technology Demonstrations on 334 hectares in fifteen governorates, 128 farm families are establishing plots with new crop varieties for extension field days.; Kirkuk Veterinary Hospital Renovation: fifty communities will benefit from a $96,000 grant to renovate a hospital that serves more than 100,000 livestock in the area; Taza and Rashad Veterinary Clinic Rehabilitation: a $50,000 grant will be matched by supplies and equipment from the Ministry of Agriculture. These rural clinics are the two principal sources of vaccines and medicines for animals in 125 local communities; Internet connectivity and repairs to the Baghdad University School of Agriculture will receive a $75,000 grant that will benefit 4,509 students; seven grants, totaling $394,000, to build the capacity of Iraq's agriculture sector, emphasizing veterinary programs allows an immediate, highly visible response to the challenges that face herders and farmers; Ministry of

Agriculture is establishing eighteen date palm nurseries throughout Iraq in support of its goal to reestablish Iraq's dominant position in the international date market, a position it lost under the former regime. Dates are a national treasure for Iraq with both symbolic and economic significance. This project, which received support and technical assistance from USAID, helped ensure the preservation of Iraq's 621 varieties of date palm.

Marshlands: Construct environmental, social and economic base-lines for the remaining and former marshlands, assist marsh dwellers by creating economic opportunities and viable social institutions, improve the management of marshlands, and expand restoration activities; promote wetlands restoration and provide social and economic assistance to marsh dwellers.

As of March 2004: Created a hydraulic model of the marshes to improve water management; equipped a soil and water quality lab at the new Center for Iraq Marshlands Restoration implementing pilot projects to improve treatment of waste and drinking water; provided social-economic assistance through job – and income-generating activities in fisheries, aquaculture, livestock production, and date-palm reproduction; monitored water quality in re-flooded sites; extended healthcare services to marsh dwellers; built local capacity by partnering with the Ministry of Water Resources, the Ministry of the Environment, the University of Basrah College of Agriculture, the AMAR Charitable Trust, and the Iraq Foundation, and the governments of Canada, Italy, the United Kingdom, and Australia.

Improve Efficiency and Accountability of Government
Local Governance: Promoted diverse and representative citizen participation in provincial, municipal and local councils, strengthened the management skills of city and provincial administrations, local interim representative bodies, and civic institutions to improve the delivery of essential municipal services, promoted effective advocacy and participation of civil society organizations, enhancing leadership skills, and serving as a recruiting tool for future leaders.

As of March 2004: Implemented local governance activities in eighteen governorates with more than 20 million Iraqis engaged in policy discourse through local government entities and civil society organizations to: enhance transparency and participation in local decision-making processes; restored basic services; improved the effectiveness of local service delivery; established and expanded the number of civil society organizations that interact with local government entities; established sixteen governorate councils, seventy-eight district councils, 192 city or sub-district councils, and 392 neighborhood councils; awarded $13.4 million to government agencies and civil society organizations to strengthen the capacity of municipal authorities to deliver core municipal services; committed $2.4 million to support the CPA's nationwide Civic Education Campaign; supported preparation of 2004 city council budgets in Mosul, Al Hillah, Babil, and An Najaf; recruited and trained more than 400 democracy facilitators.

Transition Initiatives: Building and sustaining Iraqi confidence in the transition to a participatory, stable, and democratic Iraq and working closely with the CPA, USAID's Iraq Transition Initiative assists Iraqi NGOs, national government institutions, and local governments to increase Iraqi support for the transition to sovereignty through quick-dispersing, high impact small grants.

As of March 2004: Awarded 645 small grants totaling more than $43 million for quick impact activities that support good governance, civil society, conflict management and mitigation, and human rights and transitional justice; supported initiatives crucial to the democratic transition, including civic education, civil society and media development, increased women's participation, conflict mitigation, and transitional justice. Groups targeted for assistance included women's and youth groups, professional associations, and human rights organizations; met critical needs after the conflict by providing short-term employment, restoring basic government and community services, increasing Iraqi access to information and communication, and encouraging protection of human rights; awarded two grants worth $475,000 to the Ministry of Human Rights for the rehabilitation of buildings to house the National Evidence Storage Facility (NESF). The NESF will serve as a venue to analyze recovered documents and store forensic evidence of mass graves and human rights abuses of the Ba'ath government.

Community Action Program: Promoting diverse, representative citizen participation in and among communities to identify and meet critical community needs utilizing local resources. CAP was implemented by five US NGOs with offices in nine major Iraqi cities. Each concentrated on one region in Iraq: ACDI/VOCA (North), International Relief and Development—IRD (Baghdad), Cooperative Housing Foundation International—CHF (Southwest Central), Mercy Corps (Southeast Central), and Save the Children (South).

As of March 2004: Established more than 650 Community Action Groups in sixteen governorates. The projects undertaken by these groups were part of a campaign targeting grassroots democratic development; CAP committed $49.2 million for 1,365 community projects across Iraq; eight hundred projects have been completed; Iraqi communities have contributed $15.8 million to community projects, including labor, land, buildings, and other in-kind assistance; ACDI/VOCA focused on the conflict prone areas of Mosul, Kirkuk, the area northwest of Baghdad, and the Iran-Iraq border. One hundred forty-one completed projects and another 144 in development. These included establishing a youth center in Huwija and establishing a new local water supply in Tikrit; CHF established a strong presence in the communities of the Shi'a holy cities of Najaf and Karbala, as well as Hillah by establishing active community associations. An emphasis on critical infrastructure provided these communities with access roads, sewage and water rehabilitation, school repairs, and swamp clean-up in addition to vital social infrastructure such as community centers and sports clubs. Ninety-nine projects completed; IRD completed 200 projects with another 105 projects in development. IRD focused increasingly on income and employment generation to address these critical needs around Baghdad; Mercy Corps completed eighty-nine projects and had ninety-three more in development. These projects focused on water, sewage, community clean-up, and school rehabilitation; Save the Children completed 271 projects in the south, which include about forty percent female membership. Projects focused on immediate community needs such as sewage clean up, water treatment and distribution, public health, and girls' access to education.

CPSIA information can be obtained
at www.ICGtesting.com
Printed in the USA
LVHW110125221020
669488LV00009B/965

9 781948 598330